Ten. Sam

Island
Anchieta
Rebellion, the Truth and the Legends

Island Anchieta
Rebellion, the Truth and the Legends

Graphic Design and Layout	Journalist Cleyton Carlos Torres
Cover	Anísio Vila Nova Jr.
Illustration	Renato França
Photos	Samuel Messias de Oliveira Fernando Cataçuba
Revision in portuguese	Samuel Messias de Oliveira Prof. Sub. Ten. Aparecido da Silva Dr³ Mara Cristina Pereira de Oliveira Prof³ Bete Guimarães Journalist Cleyton Carlos Torres
Translation	Georgia Morgan

O484i   Oliveira, Samuel Messias de
          Island Anchieta - Rebellion, the Truth and the Legends / Samuel Messias de Oliveira. - - Pindamonhangaba, SP: Autor, 2010.
          176 p. ; 21 cm.

        ISBN 978-85-905167-4-3

        1. Literatura. I. Oliveira, Samuel Messias de. II. Título.

                                                               CDD: 869

Copyright ® 2011 by Samuel Messias de Oliveira

Is expressly forbidden to reproduce all or part of this work, by any means or process, without prior permission of the author.

Lieutenant Samuel Messias

Opening remarks

The State park of Ilha Anchieta

What can I say about this island which at times makes me feel free and, at others, like I am a captive?

Free, because I can breathe this special air, with its smell of vegetation and sea.....Free, because I can look at the horizon and wonder at the scenery and the colours of the sea and the sky.

Captive, because I like to share in its relaxed air, the feeling of security one feels there and its music.

Yes, there is always a certain kind of music that makes our island feel enchanted, night and day. There is always the music of the sea.

In this song and in this music a choir of many voices chants a hymn of faith and love for the island. I understand that it is the strength of this "song" that makes our island's history and brings it to life.

Dr^a Maria de Jesus Robim

Preface

When I became the police commander in Pindamonhangaba, I hadn't had much experience of military police work since I had been mainly concerned with public disasters, working in the area of the civil defence of Sao Paulo.

During the first few days of my new job, I asked each of my subordinates to introduce themselves and say what they did. This is when I met Lieutenant Samuel. The first meeting between two people is always a bit strange. Samuel, with his radio announcer's voice said, "I am in charge of public relations", and I replied, "well, that's what the military police certainly needs!" From then on, there was a series of developments, in Samuel's professional and private life, culminating, I would say, in this work of history.

To remind people about a tragedy is difficult for both the author and the reading public, due to the psychological necessity to re-live the history written about. The rebellion in the prison of Ilha Anchieta, despite having taken place nearly fifty years ago, is of supreme importance today, as we can see that nothing has fundamentally changed; the spectre of this tragedy stayed with the people who had lived through it, but with no-one else – it was forgotten. We can see that the authorities, from that decade to this, have treated the matter irresponsibly and with contempt. The neglect into which Ilha Anchieta fell for the last fifty years confirms the famous saying (of George Santayana)"Those who cannot remember the past are condemned to repeat it".

My friend and brother, Samuel, has retrieved the history of Ilha Anchieta from the Age of Discovery to the present day in this book. Our country, commemorating 500 years since its discovery by the Portuguese, has been well served by this book, "Ilha Anchieta, Rebellion, Facts and Legends".

Although I have not known Lieutenant Samuel for very long, I have been given the honour of writing the Preface for this book, and am extremely grateful to have been given this opportunity. At times, in the work we carry out, we are misunderstood by others; this preface is attempting to say that great works are not always made as a result of great moral purpose, or edification, but rather in the little things that life has to give. This small detail of a book, the Preface, lets us see how clever Samuel has been to bring so much together in this book, an unprecedented story, but one which, until now, was hidden in some dusty archive, which prevented its importance being appreciated.

The case of the mutiny in the Ilha Anchieta prison, despite having been the subject of various books and even a film, has not been judged important enough for the authorities to pre-occupy themselves with the justice and prison system in Brazil. As long as we continue to have a medieval structure, basically unchanged since we were colonized, we will continue to be thought of as a third world country.

It's not enough for the Human Rights organisations here in Brazil to show the bad side of the Military Police of the State of Sao Paulo and believe that they are responsible for the all the terrible things which are going on, we must look back at history and, starting from there, decide what would be best for the country.

Revenge can only lead to chaos. With this book, Lieutenant Samuel shows that, with humility and determination, the situation can improve for everyone.

I wish to finish by saying that I hope this work serves as a framework for investigating our country's history, so that our future can be a better one.

Congratulations to Samuel and his wife Mara for this brilliant piece of research and their dedication to our ideals of hard work and fraternity.

Pindamonhangaba 15th December 1999

Eugênio Cesário Martins
Captain Military Police

Dedicatória

À minha esposa Mara Cristina.
Aos meus filhos Luzia, Sandra, Saulo, Davi e Guilherme.
À minha nora Gabriela.
Aos meus genros Julio César e Fernando.
Aos meus netos Camila, Felipe, Julinho, Lucas, Gabriel, Gustavo e Maria Eduarda.
À sobrinha Lya Aline.
À minha sogra Dayse.
A todos meus familiares que se foram e aos que estão neste plano.
E, finalmente, àqueles que fazem segurança nas noites frias e chuvosas, com o risco da própria vida, fugindo de Morfeu, enquanto a população em seus braços dorme...

Ilha Anchieta
Historical background

The first known owner of the island was the cacique Cunhambebe, the most powerful of the leaders of the Tupinamba tribe. We know all about him thanks to the work of Padre Anchieta, who tried to bring peace between the Portuguese and the native people of the coast, the Tamoios, leading later to the meeting of the indigenous peoples later known as the "Confederation of the Tamoios".

At that time the island was known as "Tapera de Cunhambebe" and, in the natives own language as Po-Qua, which means pointed. It is believed this refers to the two mountains at the two ends of the island, Morro do Papagaio (Parrot's Peak) and Morro do Farol (Lighthouse Peak).

During the seventeenth and eighteenth centuries no mention of the island can be found.

1800 - the island, still called Ilha dos Porcos, gave shelter to a detachment of the Portuguese army, who were probably hoping to guarantee possession of the island.

1850 - The British navy established a base on the island in order to prevent the slave ships from Africa reaching the coasts of Brazil to unload their slaves, now that this practice had been declared illegal under international law.

1885 - on the 21st April of that year, a Provincial law (number 11) created the parish of the Lord Jesus of the Ilha dos Porcos. According to documents pertaining to public education in Sao Paulo, at that time the island had a school with more than thirty boys. This shows how developed a place it was.

1893 - a law against vagrants and idlers was passed.

1902 - On the 10th of October of that year a law authorised the setting up of a correctional centre in a place yet to be chosen, to be under the command of the Ministry of Home Affairs and Justice.

1904 - The first steps were taken to establish a "Colonia Correcional do Porto das Palmas" on Ilha dos Porcos in order to "round up men considered to be vagrants or idlers". (The correctional facility for minors would only be established thirty years later, in Taubate).

1908 - The Porto das Palmas prison was opened in January of that year... (na Ilha dos Porcos) "mandada construir pelo Governo do Estado, sendo Presidente do Estado o Exmo. Sr. Dr. Jorge Tibiriçá; Secretário de Justiça os Exmo. Srs. José Cardoso de Almeida e Washington Luiz Pereira de Souza. Projeto de engenharia do Dr. Ramos de Azevedo. Construtor o Engenheiro Luiz Teixeira Leite". This information can still be seen on the marble slab on the front of the administration building of the prison.

1914 - the distance from the mainland and from the capital meant that the upkeep of the prison was both expensive and difficult, and so the gaol was closed and the prisoners transferred to the correctional facility in Taubate or the Fazenda Modelo (both in the Paraiba valley).

1914 - the island was leased to Agostinho Rossi, who hired fishermen and farmers who moved there and populated the island. They worked for Rossi, who planned to set up a small fishing industry and promote agriculture.

1919 - The (state) president, Altino Arantes, disembarked on the island when he was visiting this part of the coast (Litoral Norte) and, when he had seen the situation there for himself, decided to rescind the contract made with Rossi. However, it was found to be necessary to send police officers from Ubatuba to dislodge the tenant who did not want to leave.

1920 - Dr Oscar Dutra e Silva arrived on the island to establish a refuge from foot and mouth disease in order to protect the health of the animals in the state of Sao Paulo. He took with him Armando Meira Bohn, who stayed on as caretaker after the refuge had been closed. During his time as caretaker he was given a yearly allowance with which he paid native people to look after the island.

Dr Armando Maria Bohn got married in Ubatuba and lived there until his death.

1926 - the state govenment did not know what to do with two

thousand Russian immigrants who were being held in Mooca and so they transported them to the island. This was reported in the local newspaper, the "Cidade de Ubatuba" on the 23rd May under the headline "Hospedaria dos Imigrantes".

The state government is making use of the Ilha dos Porcos by setting up a hostel for immigrants there. The director of the hostel is the illustrious gentleman Joao Tobias Filho and the island is home to the garrison of the 1st Brigade consisting of privates, two corporals and two sergeants, under the command of first lieutenant Alcides do Valle.

Dr Boanerges Pimenta has recently been named as the doctor in charge of the health of the 2,000 immigrants. It is thought that the Russian immigrants will not stay on the island for very long.

It is not known who the beautiful woman is who has accompanied them as an interpreter.

The men who came to the island at the time of Armando Bohn left when the immigrants arrived.

The plantations they left helped feed the immigrants, who did not know that cassava can be poisonous if the milk of the cassava is not expelled before it is made into flour. Thus it was reported in the Notary Public in Ubatuba that the death of one Vasili Topalo, 26, on 23rd April 1926 was due to cassava poisoning.

On 1st August of the same year, another 150 deaths were registered in the same notary public's archive, by Luiz Passos Junior, who had stayed on as caretaker when the immigrant hostel closed. All the deaths had been certified by the doctor, Boanegres Pimenta. According to Jorge Cocicov in his book "Immigration to Brazil; Bulgarians and Russians", there were twenty other causes of death apart from that of cassava toxicity, which shows the dire medical situation on the island at this time. The same author claims that the doctor Boanegres Pimenta was only appointed long after the first deaths. Those immigrants who did survive their time on the island were returned to Santos by boat.

1929 - the State government passed a statute re-opening the prison on Ilha dos Porcos, but, despite the fact that officials had been appointed and plans made, the re-opening of the prison did not take place that year.

1930 - the coup which brought Getulio Vargas to power resulted in a large number of arrests. Since there were not enough places to imprison all those who had rebelled against him, the island was once more pressed into service, and the "Presidio Politico de Ilha dos Porcos" was established.

1932 - when the warship "Revolucao Constitucionalista" dropped anchor just off the island, in front of the prison, the administration panicked and the prisoners rebelled and carried out acts of vandalism. They were quickly transferred, by foot, to Taubate, a journey of some 100 kilometres which they did in four days. When the Revolution had ended the prison was re-opened, still using its old name of "Presidio Politico". In practice, however, the political prisoners, who had continued to carry out acts of rebellion, ended up staying in Sao Paulo, while the common prisoners, whose places they had taken, were transferred to the island. In this way, the prison on the island was used for all kinds of prisoners - except political ones. The prisoners on the island ranged from really dangerous ones to juveniles and to those who had never been tried, much less found guilty, but who were considered "idlers" or vagrants and had been picked up on the streets by the special constables. These vagrants were shipped every three months from the port of Santos to the island on board the ship "Itaipava". On the return voyage the ship took those prisoners who had completed their three months on the island for vagrancy or for gambling (see "O Escoteiro" further on).

At this time, the well-known reporter on the "Folha da Noite", Willy Aureli, had a suggestion to make. He had been very critical of the conditions inside the gaol, especially the fact that the prisoners were kept idle and that no attempts were made to rehabilitate them, and so he suggested that they should be used to restore the ancient imperial road which had been used by to move troops from Ubatuba to Taubate transforming it into a road which could be used by vehicles.

This recommendation was approved by the Prison Director, Major Newton Feliciano dos Santos and by the mayor Aristides Bonifacio Garcia, and the order to begin work on the road was given.

Major Newton sent a group of prisoners from the island, a military escort and food. The town of Ubatuba provided tools and materials.

The road had reached the two kilometre mark, rising from Ubatuba up the mountainside, when the work had to be abandoned because of the Constitutional Revolution. Later the construction of the road was resumed by an engineer from the State Department for Roads, Dr Mariano Montesanti.

1934 - on 19th March the name of the island was changed to that of Ilha Anchieta, commemorating the fourth centenary of the birth of Padre Jose de Anchieta. The name of the penitentiary was therefore changed to the Political Prison of Ilha Anchieta.

1942 - in this year it became a maximum security prison and its name was changed yet again this time to Instituto Correcional de Ilha Anchieta (ICIA).

1945 - a group of Japanese, known as Shindo Renmei, were sent to the island as political prisoners. They were Japanese who had killed those of their compatriots they considered to be traitors for accepting that Japan had lost the Second World War. The members of Shindo Renmei insisted on obedience to the Emperor and would allow no talk of failure in the war. President Vargas sent them to Anchieta, swelling the numbers there to 950. The island had never had such an abundance of fruit and vegetables as it did when so many Japanese were imprisoned there! They were very obedient and there were no problems with discipline. (The book "Coracoes Sujos" by Fernando Moraes deals with this episode).

1952 - on the 20th June there took place what became known as the largest prisoner rebellion in the world. The Ilha Anchieta rebellion became even more well known because an Italian film director came to Brazil and contracted Tonia Carrero, Costinha and the Argentinian Arturo de Cordova to make the movie "Maos Sangrentas" (Blood on His Hands) about the leader of the rebellion, Joao Pereira Lima.

1952 - After the rebellion, the prisoners who had taken part in it were tried on the island itself in a court which had been specially established for that purpose.

1955 - The Director of the Prison, Paulo Vianna, and the Lieutenant

Jonas Simoes Machado decided to transfer all the prisoners to the mainland; the ones who were considered the most dangerous were taken to Taubate and the others to the Instituto de Reeducacao de Tremembe. The prison on Ilha Anchieta was closed.

1955 - in September the soldier Xavier was left in charge of the island and he was later succeeded by his son Valdinei Xavier, who remains on the island to this day.

1977 - the island was declared to be a State Park, with the name Parque Estadual da Ilha Anchieta (PEIA), under the administration of the state government for the Environment, with the aim of preserving the buildings considered to be of historical interest, protect the environment and offer scientists a place where they could pursue their studies as well being used as a place for cultural events.

At the present time the agronomist Dr Viviane Buchianeri and Mrs Heloisa Folegatti are in charge of protecting the island's historical and cultural heritage.

Private José Benedito da Silva, responsible for the payment and correspondence of the soldiers on the island. (1947)

The Island Garrison on the patio of the barracks. (1947)

Private José Benedito da Silva also helped guard the island. (1947)

Military Barracks of Ilha Anchieta. (1947)

Garrison of the Prision Barracks. (1947)

Soldiers of the Military Attachment of Ilha Anchieta. (1947)

The boat "Ubatubinha", briging provisions from Santos to the prison on Ilha Anchieta. (1947)

Coincidences

a) Sign of Design

I was born at number 203, Rua Benjamim Constante, in the centre of Itatiba, in the state of Sao Paulo. My entry to the world took everyone by surprise; my mother was 43 at the time and her youngest child, my beautiful sister Clara, was already 18. When I was two we went to live in a neighbourhood of Itatiba called Paula Abreu. Our house was a small one, just like all the others on that street. Not only did we have financial problems at that time, but also many health issues.

I was a child who was very sensitive to the energy around us. Frequently I would feel energy whirling around my head, as if playing with me. It would upset me when I felt this energy making its way to my father who, sitting in a chair by the sitting-room door, was completely unaware of what I could feel. I would beg my mother to prevent this energy from upsetting my father but she, though sensitive herself, could not see or feel what I could. Eventually, the spirits would disappear.

We lived in Paula Abreu until I was four, when we moved to Pindamonhangaba. My brother-in-law, Benedicto Chagas Soares, much older than his wife, my sister Clara, gave her a smallholding at 140, Rua Cardoso, where I was brought up. I was five when my father died from complications with diabetes.

As I grew up the visions that I had had in Itatiba did not return until one day a lady that we liked very much, Dona Sinha, came to play with me in front of our house, where I was sitting with my sister Clara. Dona Sinha danced, sang and asked me to get rid of a large tick which had settled on her face. When I tried to remove it I realised it was a freckle and she laughed at my surprise and went off home. Sinha lived in a humble, brick house, with four rooms and a roof made from mud tiles, typical of the ones found in the state of Sao Paulo at that time. Sinha had one son, Geraldinho, who had already grown up and left home to work. Dona Sinha's husband was bed-ridden. People said he had "a stomach full of water" and I, by now five or six, was terrified of him. Although we had been living in Pindamonhangaba for more than a year I had never seen him out of bed. When Dona Sinha left me laughing the day I have mentioned, I had a strong premonition and said to my sister Clara:

- "Poor lady! Little does she know that tomorrow a coffin will be leaving her house."

My sister got angry with me and told me off:

- "What on earth has made you say that?! Where do you get these ideas from?"

I was frightened they were going to give me a slap for what I had said and so I ran off down the back of our land and hid in the bushes until I was sure they weren't after me.

The next day I was walking through the kitchen where my mother was washing the dishes and my sister drying them, when I heard Clara say:

- "Can you believe, Mum, that Samuel said a coffin would be taken from Dona Sinha's house today and her husband has just dropped dead?"

Once again I ran off to hide at the bottom of the garden!

When I was seven, my mother gave me a small green wooden truck with the words "Expresso Anchieta" written in white along the sides. I remember I wasn't very fond of this truck, preferring the ones belonging to Milyom Aneas who was two years older than me, He liked to show off his toys, as kids do, showing me the truck with "Expresso Patricio" and another "Expresso Brasileiro".

My brother in law died and my sister married again. Her new husband, Joao Batista Guimaraes, became like a second father to me.

Much later, in 1969, I was assigned to the Guard Battalion, in Rua Jorge Miranda, near where the Tiradentes underground station in Sao Paulo is today. What a coincidence that this battalion is now called the 2nd Anchieta battalion.

I stayed in the capital of Sao Paulo for ten years, and a year or so before I was transferred to the interior of the state I happened to be killing time in the library when I came across a book called "Motim da Ilha (Mutiny on the Island), about Ilha Anchieta, of course.

The following year I was transferred to the 5th BPMI in Taubate and went to work in the Instituto de Reeducacao in Tremembe, where prisoners would serve out the last two years of their sentences. This small town is located between Taubate and Pindamonhangaba, where family of mine still live.

Some of my new colleagues were quite a lot older than me and nearly all of them had a lot more experience in the police force. Several of them had worked on Ilha Anchieta.

One day some soldiers of the fifth battalion came to the institute in Tremembe. They had just graduated and were waiting to be sent to their first posts as PMs (Military Police). When I saw them waiting outside in the patio of the prison I went over and asked them if they knew where they going and they gave me the names of a number of places. I particularly remember one soldier, Valdinei.

He told me he was going to Ilha Anchieta to take over from his father, Soldier Xavier, who had been working there for 25 years and who was only waiting for his son to arrive in order to retire. (Valdinei did take over and remains on the island to this day).

In the IRT, the old Fazenda Modelo, guard duty, patrolling the walls, was 24 x 48, that is, 24 hours on duty followed by 48 hours off. During those 24 hours we had 3 hours on the walls followed by 3 hours free but we had to remain within the perimeter boundary as we could be called on at any time. On hot nights, we used to get together during our time off from patrolling and sit together on the ground or on the wooden bench in front of the Detachment and chat. Sometimes, interesting things were said.

It was mainly the old guys who liked telling stories and the name of Ilha Anchieta often cropped up. If the night was cold we would make a bonfire and it would start off slowly but gradually warm us up, and we would take along tin jugs of hot coffee and buttered rolls to accompany our story-telling, munching along to the stories of the past.

I remember one soldier, Iracino, (the "pio") reminiscing about the trip across the water from Saco da Ribeira in Ubatuba to Ilha Anchieta. The trip was always made in canoes, rowing, and if any soldier were to be silly enough to trail his hand through the water he would be warned to stop by the boatman who would say:

- "Careful, mate, the "tintureira" will snap your arm right off if you do that!"

Iracino explained that the tintureira was a kind of shark that was very common in those parts of the sea near the island.

One day I noticed that the garrison of the detachment of the military guard seemed to be worried about something. There was a heavy, almost funereal kind of atmosphere...

I asked one of the "old guys":

- Why are you all so quiet? What's going on?
- Don't you know who has arrived here as a prisoner?
- No!
- João Pereira Lima.
- So what? We've already got 200 prisoners, what difference does one more make?

It makes a huge difference! He was the leader of the Ilha Anchieta rebellion...

I said nothing more as I considered that the "old guy" must have his reasons for being so worried and that the least I could do was to go along with him. I also remembered that book I had read in Sao Paulo, "O Motim da Ilha" by Dr Benedito Nunes Dias, and I began to wait for something to happen too...

In the evenings, when the sun began to set behind the Serra da Mantiquera, I used to observe Joao Pereira Lima walking by himself in the patio of the IRT. He was about 1,80m tall and around 60 years old with grey hair, imposing without being arrogant in any way. He used to smoke very elegantly, always using a cigarette-holder, and kept his packet of cigarettes in a cigarette case tucked inside his waistband, on the left. He always walked about by himself. Whenever another prisoner would come up to talk to him, they would stop about three metres away and ask permission to come closer. Pereira Lima would raise one of his hands and make a gesture inviting the other man to come up to him. The prisoner would respectfully say whatever he had to say and Pereira Lima would reply seriously, either nodding or shaking his head, yes or no. He never said anything or did anything else. He would insist on the police officer on duty being able to witness everything. He didn't want any problems. They had already got everything they wanted from him. He had been known the world over. He was a "big beast" in the underworld. His story had been so well known outside Brazil that an Italian film director had come to Brazil and had made a film called "Maos Sangrentas" with Tonia Carrero, Costinha and an Argentinian actor called Arturo de Cordova, as well as 500 extras, about the leader of the Ilha Anchieta rebellion. The film was made in Portuguese with Italian subtitles and the original is Italy. It took me five years to get my hands on a copy.

There is now a copy in the museum collection on the island. Soon afterwards, in 1982, I was promoted to Corporal and was transferred from the IRT just when Pereira Lima was released. I never saw him again.

b) How I got interested in the rebellion

In about 1976 when I was in the Military Police and worked in the second company of the second battalion of the Transport Police in Rua Desembargador Vicente Penteado, 70, Jardim Paulistano, Capital de São Paulo, Captain Geraldo Sophia, helped by 1º Sgt Silvio Modesto Pereira, 2º Sgt Panosso, 3º Sgt Pereira, Cb Uerba, Sd Admir e Sd Mauro, set up a library to help those police officers who had some free time or who were being disciplined to while away the time. I was living near Pico do Jaragua, which, while officially part of the capital, was kilometres away from where I worked and I had to take three different buses to get there. The journey was always interesting... (a lot of work for the road).

During my time off, waiting for my weekend shift, I would

spend my time reading. One day I came across something I would never forget - the book Motim da Ilha written about police chief Nicolau Ulrico Mario Centola, who had been on the Litoral Norte (coast of Sao Paulo state) helping to catch the prisoners who had escaped from the island of Anchieta during the famous rebellion of 1952.

I never thought that this book would come to have so much importance for me later on in my life. There were so many books, so many different stories. The library was looked after by Ademir, soldier 34 214, a young, competent police officer and an excellent motorbike rider who lived in the barracks. His work was out in the streets riding around on a 350cc police motorbike but he became our librarian in his spare time. I never knew if this was his own idea or not. Let me elaborate. Our captain was a bit of a bully. Weak people could be taken advantage of.

Returning to my own life; in 1977, I took advantage of a helping hand from Colonel Helio Guaycuru de Carvalho who was a cousin of my old science teacher, Eduardo San Martin, and, after nearly ten years in São Paulo, accomplished what had been a dream of mine; I was given a transfer to the 5th battalion of the Military Police, "General Salgado", in Taubaté, working in the IRT in Tremembé, where, in those days, the prisoners saw out the last two years of their sentences.

Arriving there, I found myself in heaven-on earth.

My Commander was a 3rd sergeant, almost German in appearance, 1.80 m tall, slender, blonde with blue eyes and a cool air of the intellectual about him. His name was Wilson Kunzler Nicolini. When I first saw him I thought I had jumped out of the frying pan into the fire; I had escaped Captain Sophia only to fall into the hands of this "nazi" who was sure to be a stickler for discipline! As time went on, I realised that he was not at all like he had seemed at first sight. He was both mother and father to his subordinates. He did all he could to protect us from the pitfalls of professional life and sometimes even took the rap for mistakes that he hadn't in fact made himself. He did this because he lamented the fact that the regulations were inflexible; no errors were ever overlooked or forgiven, not even minor ones, or ones due to carelessness.

So, there in the IRT, I got to know some of the old guard, the ones who were about to retire, and, on moonlit nights we would sit around and chat, sometimes round a bonfire, and I would get to hear stories about Ilha Anchieta.

I spent five years in that prison until one day Sergeant Nicolini pulled me aside and said "I have shared a lot with you here in this gaol but you, Samuel, in particular should not waste your life away here in this freezing hole…….you should make a proper career for yourself. You are wasting your talents here if you don't try to become a corporal. To be a corporal, a sergeant and see how far you can get. If nothing else, you'll have a bit more money to spend in the supermarket. A bit more food to put on the table for your family. These things make a difference to what you can afford. Take what I am saying seriously before it's too late".

I felt flattered but, even so, replied, "Sorry, but I'm not interested. I spent ten years in the southern neighbourhoods of Sao Paulo and saw ten of my colleagues get killed and another Lieutenant Pinati, left a paraplegic in a wheelchair, and, apart from that, I went through some really bad times. If I am promoted to corporal I will almost certainly have to go back to Sao Paulo and I am happy here in Pindamonhangaba with my wife and children, I don't want to go back there".

As I had returned to my studies and finished secondary school, I was waiting to do the entrance exam to study law at university, which was my aim in life. At the same time, I had set up some beehives in the grounds of the prison and, together with Sergeant Nicolini and Corporal Gileno, began to raise bees and collect their delicious honey, right there in the IRT. When the sergeant needed someone to type for him, I offered my services and did that too.

One morning when I arrived for work the Sergeant called me over and said "It looks as if you're going to have to be locked up!". I had no idea why until he explained to me that a telegram had arrived from São Joseé dos Campos asking for the names of those people who wanted to do the "concurso", the open competition, to become corporal, and that he had taken it upon himself to put my name forward and sent the report to the Local Police command. If I didn't now enrol it would cause all kinds of problems, letters, demands for explanations etc and would look really bad that I had shown interest then changed my mind, and this would probably result in my incarceration....at least for a few days!

Facing this problem, and seeing just how determined the Sergeant was, I decided to play for time and said I would need a month's leave to study, seeing that the exam was a difficult one. He gave me a stern look and said, "OK, leave now, consider yourself on vacation". That very same day I went to Sao Jose dos Campos and registered for the exam to be promoted to Corporal.

When I had finished the course to become corporal in Rio Pequeno, near Osasco, in May 1982, I returned to the IRT in Tremembe. It was at this time that Joao Pereira Lima was coming to the end of his sentence for having killed the Director of the Sao Jose prison in Rio Preto.

After four months as corporal in the IRT, I was transferred to Pindamonhangaba, where I stayed another four months waiting to be accepted on the course to become sergeant in the famous Centro de Formacao e Aperfeicoamento de Pracas (CFAP) in Sao Paulo. Once accepted, I stayed there for seven and a half months and then returned to Pindamonhangaba when the course finished in September 1983. I took over the command of the military detachment in Redencao da Serra and worked there for the next two years. After that, I swapped jobs with Sergeant Amauri, and went to work at the CCTT . This was a maximum security prison where the most dangerous of the Ilha Anchieta rebel prisoners had been taken in September 1955 and where, almost nine years later, they set fire to the place, burning down the Alcantara Machado Wing on 14 August 1961, and they ended up dying there.

The reader of this book will surely appreciate how throughout my life there have been links between me and Ilha Anchieta, a link which began when I first came across the book, "Motim da Ilha". These links became even stronger when, in February or March 1998, I became a member of the Association of Reserve Officials of the Military Police (AORPM). Speaking about the island one day with Captain Wilson Pardo Palma, President of the Taubate section of the AORPM, I discovered that he was the husband of Dona Gracia, Soldier Joao Caetano de Oliveira's daughter. Dona Gracia had lived for many years on Ilha Anchieta when she was a child. Further on in this book the reader will see what her life was like on the island before the rebellion.

A little while after this conversation with Captain Palma, one Sunday afternoon, my wife Mara and I drove out to the Bairro do Pouso Frio in Pindamonhangaba. We had no particular reason, just to relax and enjoy the beautiful afternoon. We stopped at the top of a hill to enjoy the view. We had pulled over at the side of the road and were able to hear two men talking near a cowshed. They were installing a sugar cane cutter. We couldn't hear what they were saying; all we were interested in was looking at the mountains, enjoying the breeze coming down from the forest and listening to the birds as the sun was setting.

We suddenly heard a shout. It was one of the men inviting us to come over. I gave Mara a look as if to ask what she thought and she smiled back as if to say "Come on, we have got nothing to lose". I parked the car by the entrance to the farm and we made our way to the cowshed. Thus we met the owner, Waltinho Cardoso, and the caretaker, Sr Joao. Once the cutter had been installed, Waltinho invited us in to have a coffee. As we talked, we found out that Waltinho was the son of Corporal Walter, one of the soldiers who had fought bravely against the rebels until he had had to surrender when he ran out of ammunition. Together with his colleagues, he was kept inside the prison until reinforcements from the Taubate battalion arrived. More can be read about this episode in the chapter "Rebellion".

Waltinho's mother, Dona Aydee Cardoso, who had not been married long at that time, went over to the neighbours' house while her husband was fighting the rebels and there, crying, but trying to be brave, they resisted the rebels as well as they could. Details of this are to be found later on in this book in Dona Aydee's own words.

So, we spent a really nice evening in our new friends' house, and we left promising to meet again and to talk more about the rebellion, this time with Waltinho's mother.

In May of the same year, 1998, I found out that Under-Lieutenant Sodre, President of the Taubate Association of Under-Lieutenants and Sergeants, was planning an excursion to Ilha Anchieta. I didn't waste any time but immediately bought two tickets, one for myself and the other for Mara, my wife. I invited Private Afonso, film-maker and social communications secretary of the fifth battalion, to come along to cover the trip.

So we went to Ilha Anchieta and I finally got to know the island.

What a wonderful feeling it was to arrive at the place I had heard so much about and to hear stories of the island from the very mouths of those who had been there in both happy times and times of terror.. We filmed everything. The excursion, the island, everything! We stayed at the holiday home of the military officers in Caraguatatuba, a wonderfully relaxed and comfortable place which no-one would be able to find fault with. We combined work with pleasure. It was a truly marvellous time. Afonso had managed to get hold of a dossier which catalogued all the reports of the officials involved in the re-capture of the prisoners and the re-taking of the island in the early hours of the 21st June 1952. Afonso and I couldn't get enough of this material and devoured it eagerly. We returned to the mainland full of ideas about how we could use this information. I published five thousand copies of my newspaper, "Police news" ("Noticias Policiais") "Special Edition" about the trip and what we had found. It aroused so much interest that a further five thousand copies were published. The editors of the coastal newspapers phoned me up every day asking for more details. They wanted to know where I had got hold of these reports and the wonderful photos which accompanied them. For this, I was indebted to Senhora Brasilina Bretherick and her daughter Maria das Gracas, who had kept, for 46 years, a magazine from that time containing several photos which I photocopied. Dona Brasilina's husband had been Private Eugenio from the island barracks. Since Afonso and I were always talking on the local radio stations, they, mother and daughter, had heard us say that we were intending to pay homage to all those who had been born, had worked or who had simply lived on the island, and whom we affectionately called "Filhos da Ilha", "Children of the Island". In response to this, these two listeners had contacted us by phone and I went to their house, in the Chacara do Visconde, in Taubate, where Sra Brasilina gave me this very special magazine.

The success of these newspapers about the history of the rebellion made Mara Cristina and me decide to talk to Colonel Nelson Francisco Duarte, Commander of the Military Police of the Vale de Paraiba and the northern Sao Paulo coast, in order to propose the setting up of a commission to recover and preserve the rich history of Ilha Anchieta. We went to his headquarters in São José dos Campos and, with a copy of our newspaper on the table, put forward our suggestion. Colonel Nelson was in complete agreement with us and suggested that we get in contact with Colonel Paulo Máximo and propose that he should be the head of the commission. And that is what we did. We also invited os presidentes e os Diretores das Associações de Classes da PM, em Taubaté, para que engrossassem as fileiras conosco. Of course, we didn't forget to invite Waltinho Cardoso and his mother, Aydee.

The first thing we thought up was an act of commemoration on 20th June 1998 of the 46th anniversary of the rebellion and of those subsequent heroic acts on that fateful day. And so, at 9.45am on the 20th June 1998 the 5th Battalion stood in formation in the patio of the barracks in Taubate. On the stage, along with the civil and military authorities of the region, was father Fred, the local parish priest, who celebrated an ecumenical Mass. Standing in front of the ranked troops were the extremely emotional "Filhos da Ilha".

Many of them, who had been children at the time of the rebellion and had then been moved away, had been separated from their friends and they had never seen each other since. Now, at over 50 years of age, they were meeting up again. They had so many things to say to one another. So many things that maybe they had wanted to say when they were children, but that now, 46 years later, they would never say. Other people would, yes, say things they wanted to now they had been given the opportunity.

We found the teacher who had first taught the children, who were now gathered here as adults, to read and write. She was able to meet up with those beloved children that she had so fiercely protected that night. She had protected them, like a wild beast who had been cornered, from the fury of the prisoners.

Making enquiries, we managed to find Henrique Antonio de Oliveira, who had been born in a cell on the night of the riot. His mother was now dead, but the midwife was there to see this baby she had delivered, now a man of 46 years working in the Ford factory of Taubate.

After the Mass, silver cards were given to the children of those heroes who had died in combat during the rebellion. In addition, a special certificate was given to each "Child of the island". There followed a minute's silence. After that, the names of the dead were read out, one by one. The bugler of the Battalion then played the saddest "Last Post" that had ever been heard there. Some people felt a bit faint but Captain Doctor Luiz Fernando Correa was there with his medical team and they helped them recover.

Straight afterwards the troop marched past in homage to the Filhos da Ilha and then Commander Paulo Maximo invited us to have lunch in the refectory belonging to the battalion. Towards the end of the meal, Private Afonso put on the videotape he had made of the excursion to the island earlier that year. We could hear children asking their parents, "Isn't that Ilha Anchieta on the TV?" and their replies of "Yes, it is!" Just that nowadays the island was lively and pretty and full of day-trippers who got off the schooners, not on the pier which still had to be rebuilt, but in inflatable dinghies, and who made their way to dry land where they would lunch on fruit which the Association had provided, in the shade of the trees.

After the lunch, Commandant Paulo Maximo, who had watched the video with us, invited us to go to Ilha Anchieta the following day, the 21st June, to leave a wreath in the little chapel of Senhor Bom Jesus in memory of the dead. Even those who had sworn they would never set foot on that island again, changed their minds and were now keen to return to the place where they had grown up.

On the 21st June they went to the island and went to the chapel to lay their wreath. But there was no chapel! In its place was a souvenir shop...oh well, 46 years had gone by.....The "Children of the Island" were quite upset about this and complained to the director of the state park, DR. Manoel de Azevedo Fontes, who, with his wife the biologist Maria, promised to look into the problem now that they had been made aware of it. (Look at "First Observation" later on).

Captain Palma, representing the Reservists Association, and his wife Gracia, together with me and my wife Mara, had a meeting with the Mayor of Ubatuba, Zizinho, and his most senior staff, as well as the local parish priest Frei Gastone. We arranged to have further meetings to solve the problem of the disappearance of the chapel on the island, and now the "capelinha" has been restored! (see later on "the opening of the Chapel").

We have even had a wedding to celebrate the chapel's re-opening. On the 18th December 1999 at 2pm, Frei Gastone Possobom, the priest of Ubatuba, celebrated the first wedding on the island in 48 years. The bride, Cintia Aparecida da Silva, and the groom, Wilson Alves dos Santos, had as their best man Lieutenant Lamosa, and as guests of honour the couple who ran the island, Manoel and Maria.

We are hoping to rebuild the ruins of our barracks, now grown over, on the Morro de Papagaio, the remains of a story, not so long ago which helps us to reflect upon the struggle between good and evil which is ever present.

II The Riots

Portuga

Let's begin by talking about the brain behind the most famous rebellion of the century.

His name: Álvaro da Conceição Carvalho Farto, or "Portuga".

One fine day "Portuga" showed up in front of Captain Sadi, at that time the director of the prison of Ilha Anchieta, and asked to be put into solitary confinement. Portuga explained that he had become aware of whisperings and strange signs amongst his cell companions, which led him to fear that they were planning to kill him, and that, for this reason he would like to be put into a cell on his own when the day's work was finished, where he would be safe.

The Director didn't suspect anything because solitary confinement was usually just for those convicted of murder and no-one would choose to go there without good reason.

And...well, there was a good reason...Portuga made this request because he wanted to be by himself in the evenings, locked away and without being disturbed, in order to meticulously plan the breakout which would turn out to make headlines all over the world.

During the day, together with his most loyal friends, Portuga put together the first link in the chain of command of the rebellion. While he had lunch with some of the other prisoners in the inside patio of the prison, he would give orders that he insisted would have to be followed at all costs.

The first set of instructions was that all the prisoners should begin to behave as nicely as possible towards the administrative staff. He called the prisoner who acted as barber for the officials and told him to find a way of being transferred to the Barracks of the military guard, where he would be able to observe the detachment's layout and make sketches which would be sent to the chief's "solitary".

French hand

The prisoner who was the barber was known as Mão Francesa; mao (hand) because of his delicate touch and Francesa (French) because he was extremely effeminate, possibly even gay.

MF followed his boss's instructions to the letter and the plan got under way.

Within the walls of the Detachment, MF began copying down all the duty rotas and observing any other details which might give useful information to the Chief Planner.

Suckling pig

The prisoner Leitão, in charge of sweeping and keeping clean the paths at the front of the prison, was a really obsequious chap, and under Portuga's instructions, became even more so. The Prison Director Sadi was a vain person and had the habit of showing off what a good shot he was. Leitao began to praise his dexterity with a gun and became quite friendly with the Director, to the extent that one day he challenged him to shoot some vultures which were flying over the island by saying " you are the best shot I have ever seen...but I want to see if you can get those crows up there with a musket." The director took up the challenge and from then on was watched and heard.... He used to shoot at the crows and get huge rounds of applause from the prisoners who would be passing by on their way to collect firewood or other chores. In that way the sound of gunfire came to be common, not causing panic or alarm as it usually would in a prison environment.

The fact is that the director really was an excellent shot and it was a shame he never took part in a shooting competition because he would have won it easily. Another instruction from Portuga was that all the prisoners should try and gain the trust of the soldiers escorting them on their daily walks to the Morro do Papagaio where they cut down firewood and carried it back for use in the prison.

Operation Trust

The prisoners were so disciplined and well behaved that the regulation 10 metre distance between the group of prisoners and their military escort gradually got shorter, 9, 8, 7 metres and by the end of two months soldiers and prisoners were walking side by side. A short time later, the two groups were chatting together like old friends. When they smoked, soldiers and prisoners would light each others cigarettes using their own, it was all very chummy... On the way back from the forest to the prison, member of the soldiers' families would often look after their weapons while the soldier tied his bootlaces, for example. Groups of people traditionally antagonistic towards one another lived peacefully side by side on the island known at that time as Devil's Island.

Portuga, beside himself with glee, felt he had the wind in his sails and became more and more confident... Prisoners were now doing all kinds of jobs in the police officers' houses. They would chop firewood, plant vegetable gardens, clear water systems, make fences, and, doing these jobs began to use the roads in the Vila Militar which had previously been out of bounds to them, with the excuse that they were short cuts......always, of course, being respectful towards the wives and daughters they encountered and playing games with the small children, playing ball, and always making sure they let the kids win...

There were 453 prisoners on the island at this time, but only about fifty soldiers, made up of civil servants, sergeants, corporals and privates. Requests to the capital to send reinforcements were not successful. Maybe the chiefs of the Forca Publica (or Military police as they are known today) thought that a rebellion could never occur there, since no-one would dare try to cross the infamous "boqueirão" which separated Ilha Anchieta from the mainland, 600 metres wide and about 42 metres deep, especially given the fishermen's frequent sightings of sharks.

As for Portuga, he told the prisoner known as Smoke (Fumaça) who worked in the storeroom, to find out on which day the boat "Ubatubinha" was due to come to the island. This was a huge barge which came once a month from the port of Santos, bringing provisions to the island, and, as such, was central to the plans for escape.

Smoke (Fumaça)

Fumaça, cleverer than most, knew his job well, and found out that D Day would be Friday 20th June, and that, if the sea was calm, Ubatubinha, also known as Santense, would be mooring on the old pier at around midday. And so the day and time were chosen.

There were still a few days left to discuss the details of the mutiny, and so Portuga got his Chiefs of staff together, the worst criminals of the country. They were all prisoners of excellence, having had wide experience of the Brazilian penal system. There was João Pereira Lima, China Show, jerico, Ildefonso, Mocoroa, Sete Dedos, Diabo Loiro. To make life even more difficult for the soldiers, the night before the planned rebellion, that is, on the 19th June, the leaders of the plan killed Flores (commonly known as Dentinho) and buried him deep in the sand of beach near the banana plantation (Praia das Palmas). When they were counted in for lunch it was noticed that one prisoner was missing. The police officers were told and they went out to look for him, as was the custom whenever this occurred.

While they were searching for Dentinho, the other prisoners mentioned to the officials and soldiers that the fugitive had been talking about escaping form the island on a raft... it was all going to plan, Portuga's plan!

The police Commander called his troops together and announced that he was sending six privates, together with "Escoteiro", one of the workers, to the mainland to look for the man they supposed had fled there... this decision reduced the number of prison officers on the island, of course, but, who was worrying about that..."the atmosphere on the island was so friendly that six soldiers here or there made no difference".

D Day

As we have seen, there were 453 prisoners serving their sentences in the Ilha Anchieta prison on that day, 20th June, and about 6.30am the military escort for the chopping and transport of firewood was formed in front of the main gate.

Sergeant Theodosio Rodrigues dos Santos was in charge and he was accompanied by Private Geraldo Braga. They took the first group of around 12 prisoners, heading for Morro do Papagaio in order to cut down firewood. Straight afterwards the second escort left the prison with 110 prisoners, making their way to Ponta da Cruz, to bring back the wood chopped down the day before.

The escort for this group consisted of only two soldiers and two prison guards, unarmed civilians. Their names were private Hilario Rosa, Private Manoel França Ayres, Helio Barros and Higino Perez.

If ten soldiers were not enough for such a large group of prisoners, imagine TWO. But it was thought that there was no risk, everyone was happy, all was sweetness and light on Ilha Anchieta...

The prisoners laughed to themselves, everything was going perfectly...Joao Pereira Lima, the prisoner most respected by the others, walked alongside Private Ayres. Suddenly, he grabbed the soldier's weapon, meeting no resistance, for the soldier had no reason to suspect that all this friendliness had been one big farce. And so the mutiny had begun! Pereira Lima tied Ayres to a tree, together with Helio Barros, the unarmed civilian worker. There was nothing they could do in the face of such unexpected aggression.

Pereira Lima told them to call Private Hilario who was marching with the group in front, and when he reached the group at the back, all the prisoners lay down on the ground and Pereira Lima, who had hidden himself behind a big rock, fired straight into the face of Hilario, who died instantly.

The civilian helper, Higino, was tied up.

As soon as the 12 prisoners who had gone to cut firewood heard the shot, the previously agreed signal for action, they overpowered their military escort using the axes which they had brought with them. They slashed at the soldiers until their foreheads caved in and they were presumed to be dead. The mutineers now had two more weapons, making three muskets and a Winchester rifle in total.

Invasion of the Detachment

After they had overpowered the escorts, the two groups of prisoners united under the command of Pereira Lima, and made their way to the detachment where the soldiers were not worried because, although they had heard the shots, they assumed it was Director Sadi shooting crows again. So, with the element of surprise on their side, the prisoners prevailed against the Military Guard without any difficulty. The prisoners had brought back bundles of wood on their shoulders as they always did, with one big difference; this time, they had hidden the arms and the axes in the middle. As they entered the barracks they jumped through the windows and murdered the soldiers they found there. Some soldiers, who were not on duty, were resting on their beds, unarmed, and were not able to get their weapons because the bandit, China Show, armed with a rifle, had strategically placed himself in front of the window of the central corridor and could see the entrance to the weapon-store perfectly and shot anyone who tried to get there.

Joao Pereira Lima had shot and killed the gunsmith, Private Otavio dos Santos, as soon as the attack on the barracks had begun. Some soldiers fought back but were killed, their names: José Eugênio Paduan, José do Carmo da Silva, José Laurindo, Bento Moreira, Benedito Damásio dos Santos e o Sargento manipulador de farmácia Melchíades Alves de Oliveira.

In total eight soldiers and two civilian workers Portugal de Souza Pacheco e Oswaldo dos Santos were killed by the bloodthirsty, vengeful mob in horrible scenes which have never been forgotten by those who survived. The prisoner João Alves dos Santos, commonly known as "Swing" was also killed in the shoot-out. The prisoners, completely out of control, broke into the weapon store and armed themselves with machine guns, muskets, rifles, revolvers, lots of ammunition, everything they could lay their hands on.

Joao Pereira Lima, the "general" of the mutiny, divided his "army" into two columns. One column, under his direct command, attacked the Director of the Prison and of the Commanding lieutenant's homes, where some soldiers and civilian workers had taken refuge. The other column, led by Geraldo Francisco de Oliveira, known as "Negrao da Cozinha", took over all the prison buildings. In an orgy of destruction they tore down the doors of the cells and the wings of the prison and set free all the prisoners.

It was total victory for the rebels, who now took over the command of the island. All the soldiers surrendered, including Lieutenant Odvaldo Silva, the commander, who had fought bravely alongside the privates, and who, when he saw his ammunition had run out, intended to die fighting, but who was persuaded by Private Chagas to give himself up. All the soldiers were rounded up, together with their families and the civilian workers, and locked up in the prison cells to await their fate.

The director Sadi, after he had run out of ways to defend himself and had surrendered, was shot by Jorge Floriano, China Show, but managed to survive. After shooting the Director, China Show made his way to the Director of Discipline's house. Portugal de Souza Pacheco, overpowered him and took him to the back of his garden where, in front of his wife and children, he was shot. The deaths of ...in the Director's back yard were attributed to ... known as Tabu.

The prison safe was broken into and all the 98,000 cruzeiros found there were stolen and divided up amongst the rebels.

At the end of the fighting there were several prisoners lying on the ground, seriously injured; these were: Benedito Rodrigues, known as "Mário Magro"; Domingos Cunha, known as "Maluco"; José da Silva, known "Zelão" e Agenor Pereira da Costa, known as "Zé Soldado" Benedito died in the boat in which he was fleeing to the mainland, and Domingos was taken to the hospital in Taubate after he had been captured but subsequently died. The other two prisoners survived. Francisco Barriento, Francisco José da Silva e Filadelfo Martins de Oliveira, also died. Sergeant Mechiades Alves de Oliveira, the prison nurse at the time of the mutiny, was helping an injured prisoner by the name of Sinval Cabral dos Santos, "Gauchão", when he was attacked by three of the rebels Alcindo Cândido Gomes, known as "Mocoroa", Nelson Garcia e Pedro Joaquim dos Santos, known as "Daziza" who beat him up terribly until Mocoroa finally turned a Schmeisser machine gun on him.

After Mechiades was murdered, Daziza kicked his face in and and attacked it with the butt of the gun leaving it completely smashed up. The civilian employee Oswaldo dos Santos, having been seriously injured by the prisoner Mocoroa, was then shot by Augusto Cordeiro Rocha (the "Bahian") and, by then near death, was attacked by Oscar Teodoro da Silva, (Mineirinho) who ran through him with a bayonet.

In the middle of this massacre, one voice made itself heard above all others;" If I hear of one woman or child being maltreated, I will kill the person responsible with my own hands….." The voice was that of Joao Pereira Lima, shouting so that everyone could hear him, and he added, "our only objective is to escape……" These are phrases which are engraved on the memories of the sixty or so survivors that we have found and form part of the island's history.

The Crossing

While Mocoroa, Daziza , China Show and other prisoners were enjoying their macabre "entertainment", Pereira Lima and Zenon Kison, "Timoshenko", tired of waiting for the big barge "Ubatubinha" which hadn't arrived, were worried about what was going to happen. They knew that there were more police out there, not just the ones on the island, who could be contacted and asked to come and help restore order. Although the prison was in flames and the radio apparatus had been destroyed, the police might have been able to communicate with the mainland, how would the rioters know……So, it was time to give up on the barge, the one that Fumaca had said was due to arrive at midday but which hadn't arrived…..Pereira Lima and Timoshenko decided to use the prison boat, the official name of which was "Carneiro da Fonte" but which was popularly known as "Bailarina" (Ballet Dancer), due to the way it would dance about on the waves, however calm the water was. Although the boat only had room for fifty people it had to take over ninety that day, who crowded onto the deck. And so it set sail in the direction of Ubatuba, passing Ponta Grossa, making for the beach of Ubatumirim, from where the rebels would make their way by land to Paraty.

It is said that the heaviest fugitives were thrown overboard to lighten the load and that they were eaten by sharks. When they got to the mainland, however, the boat ran aground on the shallow beach of Ubatubirim due to the inexperienced Timoshenko failing to slow the boat down, and it split in the middle, throwing out its evil cargo into the waves. Falling on top of one another, trampling the unlucky ones underfoot, many drowned in that desperate scramble.

Back on the island, other prisoners, not as quick as the others, managed to get hold of the canoes from the boat shed and set off for the mainland. Those who made it safe and sound to the other side reached the Ubatuba and Caraguatatuba mountains where they caused panic in the local populations. There were macabre scenes. Half-naked, starving but eager for bloodshed, the escaped prisoners had only one aim; to put as much distance between themselves and Ilha Anchieta as possible.

After the Storm

On the island, Lieutenant Odvaldo, once he had been freed by the 5th battalion (cacadores de forca publica,) took charge and re-established order on the island. He also made comfortable all the women and children who had lost their husbands and fathers and were completely disoriented. Odvaldo remained at the head of operations for the next 48 hours stopping neither to eat nor sleep.

In the middle of the rebellion Private Simao Rosa da Cunha was brave enough to swim those shark-infested waters separating the island from the mainland and arrived at Xanda beach, shivering from both the cold winter sea and exhaustion. Once he got there he took a short rest to gather his strength and then set off on a trail through the forest towards the Enseada, where he told Corporal Sudario Franco what had happened. Only then could he rest properly and he lay down on the beach, where he was helped by Chico from the Casa Maciel, a small grocer's shop which still exists.

Corporal Sudario managed to get transport from his post at Enseada to Cataguatatuba, and there, at Campo Largo, met corporal Darli, who phoned Colonel Benedito Helpidio Hidalgo, Commander of 5º Batalhão de Caçadores, in Taubate, who was responsible for the military police in the Vale de Paraiba and the Litoral Norte, and told him what had happened on the island.

The re-taking of the island

Colonel Hidalgo immediately sent troops to the coastal areas who were able to re-capture the majority of the fugitives alive, before they got over the mountain range and down into the valley of Paraiba. Given the cold, the rain and the darkness, this was not an easy task, but they managed it.

Colonel Hidalgo personally took a group of police officers from his battalion, and, at around 1.30 in the morning of the 21st June, in the cold darkness with just torches to light their way, they disembarked on Ilha Anchieta and took back the island from the rebels who had taken it over.

The rebels did not fight back. The words of Pereira Lima, and the actions of another leader who had refused to flee, kept the situation under control, and meant that no woman or child was harmed. This man was Francisco Faria Junior, who became famous and who had his sentence shortened as a reward for staying and keeping control. He left the island a free man but returned later, this time in order to work there. When he retired, he lived the rest of his life in Ubatuba. When he died a huge crowd turned out to walk behind his coffin to the cemetery where he was buried.

As for the re-capture of the island, police from Tauibate, from Santos, the Policia Fluminense and the Brazilian Army all came to help the local police re-capture the fugitives. Many prisoners died or were wounded in that battle with the men who had been sent to get them.

The brain behind the mutiny

"Portuga" was a clever man, as we have seen, and it was for this reason that he had been chosen to make the plans. He was, however, physically very weak and had many health problems to do with his heart and high blood pressure.

Although the other prisoners encouraged him to carry on running, at a certain point, when they were climbing up the Serra da Mar, he felt ill and sat down in the shade of one of the big trees, leaning against its trunk. His friends wanted to carry him but he refused to let them, and told them to continue without him, that he just wanted to rest a bit and then he would carry on. He ended up sleeping a sleep from which he would never again wake up...

He was found, days later, in that very same position, already in an advanced stage of decomposition.

The "General"

Joao Pereira Lima, the feared leader of the mutiny, who became world famous through films and books, was re-captured by a Private and a Corporal of the Platoon, under the command of Lieutenant Benedito Augusto de Oliveira, who died in Taubate in 1998...

Pereira Lima was captured when he was in the middle of having lunch with another prisoner, "Gericho", in the middle of the forest. It was all so sudden, they didn't have time to react or even to run. They were sent back to the Ilha Anchieta where they were tried along with the other fugitives. A special court was set up there, with a judge, prosecutor and lawyers, and it would remain there for three years until all the prisoners had been tried. In 1955 they were all sentenced and sent away from the island, the most dangerous to (Taubaté) and the less dangerous to the IRT in Tremembé.

Pereira Lima had his sentence commuted due to his protection of the prison officers' families during the rebellion, and, years later, was allowed to leave Carandiru and go to the Colonia Agrícola Javer de Andrade, where, however, he ended up killing the director of the prison, Instituto Penal

Agrícola Javer de Andrade…..and having passed through many penal establishments he finished his sentence in the IRT in 1982 , where the author of this book was working as a soldier (see "Chefes de revolta").

Heroes

Sargento Melchíades Alves de Oliveria;
Cabo Hilário Rosa;
Soldado Carmo da Silva;
Soldado José Eugênio Paduan;
Soldado Bento Moreira;
Soldado Benedito Damásio dos Santos;
SoldadoJosé Laurindo; e
Soldado Octávio dos Santos
Oswaldo dos Santos; e
Portugal de Souza Pachego

The Island Courthouse

As soon as the rebellion was over, the recaptured fugitives had to be put on trial. Taking into account the problems involved in moving them to Ubatuba for the trial, the government decided to try them on Ilha Anchieta itself and a special court was established.

It took three years for the sentences to be handed down; these cases always take a long time. It is interesting to note that attempting to escape, by itself, is not considered a crime in Brazil. The prisoner who succeeds in gaining his "liberty" without committing any crimes in the process (neither against the person or against property) merely loses any privileges he may have won during his time in prison. For this reason, many people think that attempting to escape is not a crime...

This courthouse remained on the island until 1955, when nearly all the trials had been concluded, and the most dangerous prisoners had been transferred to Casa de Custódia de Taubaté and the others to the IRT in Tremembé.

The island was under the command of Captain Paulo Vianna, the last director of the prison, and Lieutenant Jonas Simoes Machado, the last military commander there. The prison was closed permanently in 1955.

Only one soldier stayed on the island for the next 25 years, Private Luiz Xavier (Forca Publica). In 1977 the State Park of Ilha Anchieta was established, and it became part of the responsibility of the Secretary of State for the Environment. When Luiz Xavier (by then a sergeant) retired, he left his son, Private Xavier working in his place. At the time this book was written, he was still there.

The Book "Motim da Ilha" (Mutiny on the Island)
(Editora Soma Ltd)

Officer´s visit to Ilha Anchieta. From left to right: Major Corrêa (father of Maj. Dr. Luiz Fernando C. Corrêa; Cap. Paulo Vianna (Director of island; Cap. Oscar P. Éboli; e Tenente Jonas. (1955)

The leaders of the rebellion

Joao Pereira Lima was born in Serra Negra in the state of Sao Paulo on the 3rd February 1919. He committed his first crime at the age of 20 years, on 11th April 1939, when he murdered the Air Force sergeant Teodomiro Freitas Santos in a brothel in Sao Paulo. He was expelled from the police force, in which he had already reached the rank of sergeant, on the 20th of that month. Had it not been for this act of murder, he would probably have had a brilliant career in the police force. The Military Tribunal sentenced him to 20 years for this crime. (In the following years he removed anyone who opposed him or stood in his way, and for this reason was put in the maximum security Prison of Ilha Anchieta) Periera Lima was a man of few words but he always had a menacing smile on his face.

For the crimes carried out on Ilha Anchieta during the rebellion, Joao Pereira Lima's trial only began on 4th June 1960, nearly eight years later. He was accused of three murders, being the leader of the mutiny and of encouraging escape involving violence against the person. (The trial was not held on the island as the prison had been closed down in 1955).

The penal lawyer Dr Javier de Andrade, was one of the seven people called who spoke in Pereira Lima's defence.

At the first trial, PL was sentenced to two years and eight months of prison plus one year and five months of detention. This sentence was appealed against for being too lenient and, was increased to 30 years imprisonment. Javier de Andrade intervened on PL's behalf and managed to get him transferred to Instituto Agricola de Sao Jose de Rio Preto, where Dr Andrade was the director.

There, Pl came to be praised as a model prisoner and used as an example of how even the worst criminal could be rehabilitated. It didn't last. Just when everything seemed to be going so well, PL hit the headlines again, this time accused of having murdered Dr Javier himself, the prison director and Pereira Lima's principal protector, the man who had most faith in him and belief in his rehabilitation. For this new crime, PL received a 28 year sentence.

Later, he managed to get the two sentences to run concurrently, in accordance with article 55 of the Codigo de Processo penal. (He was released in 1982 from the jail in Tremembe, where the author of this book, then a prison soldier, had seen him).

"Mocoroa" - Alcino Candido Gomes, who had a wonderful physique, was a professional boxer before becoming involved in a life of vice. Starting off using drugs and alcohol, he drifted into a life of crime....Other criminals thought that he was a traitor, and believed that when he had been taken prisoner in the forest near Cunha he had been the one who had told the police the whereabouts of PL.

One day in the prison in Sao Paulo where he was serving his sentence, he was set upon by the other prisoners who were both judge and jury, and who condemned him to death for informing to the police. They encircled him in the patio of the prison, and one of them stabbed him through the heart with a sharp instrument and killed him.

"China Show" - Not to be confused with "China", who died during the rebellion, China Show, came from the North East of Brazil to São Paulo where he became a fire-fighter. One day he was arrested along with a band of robbers and was expelled from the fire service as a result of this. He just went downhill from then onwards and he got involved in more crimes.

He became known as "China" because of the oriental shape of his eyes and "Show" because he liked to show off his strength and provoke the prison officers in all the jails he was in. When he was given any kind of physical punishment, he was proud of how long and how much he could endure and gave a real "show"...hence his nickname.

It is hard to understand why China Show got involved in the rebellion – being Portuga's number two in the planning stage and the leader of the rebels – since he only had three months of his sentence left to serve.

He liked to do oil painting on canvas. He gave the (delegado), Dr Centola, some of his small paintings of scenes of Ilha Anchieta. His art was slightly primitivist, and he didn't have great technique with paint or solidity of colour, and there was an absence of perspective, showing that, one day he could have done pictorial art (I am grateful to Dr Benedito Nunes Dias for these comments) He was the only one we know of who managed to get through the police lines and he escaped to Salvador in Bahia, where, two years later he was recognised while he was attending mass, arrested and returned to the Ilha Anchieta, from where he was later transferred to the Penitencia do Estado de Sao Paulo.

He was moved from the Penitencia to the Casa de Detencao where he killed a fellow prisoner, no-one knows why. He became more and more out of control and was transferred to the prison mental hospital, in Franco da Rocha, where, by now completely insane, he died.

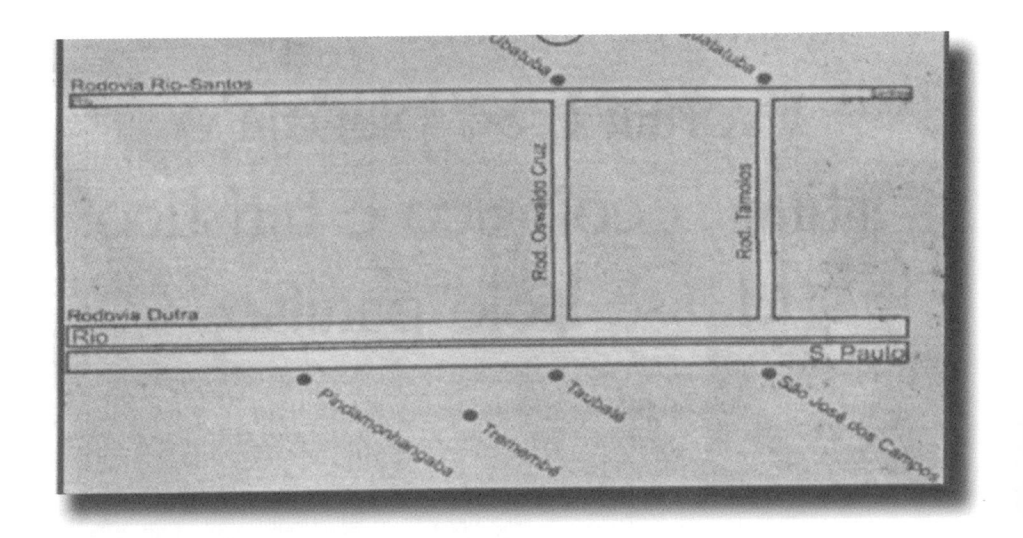

O Cruzeiro Magazine

MOTIM SANGRENTO NO PRESÍDIO DE ANCHIETA

CENAS DRAMÁTICAS DA SUBLEVAÇÃO PRESIDIÁRIA

Este soldado teve o cotovêlo esmagado num combate com os detentos. Alojado no precário hospital do Presídio, recebeu sangue. O seu estado é gravíssimo. Foi para S. Paulo.

CAP. FAUSTO SADI FERREIRA, Diretor do Presídio, que teve a sua vida garantida por Pereira Lima.

e friamente assassinados por uma horda de facínoras da pior espécie, não podemos também, por outro lado, calar a voz diante da covarde "liquidação" daqueles que, espontaneamente, capitulavam diante das autoridades. A rendição, por si só, num país medianamente civilizado, é uma garantia de vida. Não podemos também deixar de proclamar como desumano, cruel e selvagem o abandono a que ficaram relegados os sentenciados feridos. Vimos muitos dêles com o peito varado por balaços serem jogados inteiramente nus em celas imundas, sem assistência médica de qualquer espécie. E foi com pavor que, ao indagarmos do médico do 5.º B.C. da Fôrça Pública de São Paulo, sediado em Taubaté, se não ia prestar socorros a "Diabo Louro", gravemente ferido pelo Delegado de Ubatuba, ouvimos esta resposta: "Não trato de presos. Todos devem morrer a cacetadas". Concordar com tais fatos seria negar a Justiça e descrer da humanidade. Por que recusar o bálsamo à ferida de um moribundo ou massacrar um homem indefeso, que se rende, é regredir aos tempos brutos da pedra lascada.

ESTE DETENTO, localizado no Morro do Papagaio, entrega-se ao Cel. Hidalgo, Comandante do 5.º B. C., que o tratou como homem.

ESCOLTADO POR MILICIANOS de fuzil em punho, e por um detento fiel à Diretoria, vem de mãos para cima, trêmulo e amedrontado.

AO TENENTE OVIDIO dá explicações: "Dormi no mato uma noite, sòzinho. Não matei ninguém. Quis me render. Não agüentava mais".

ULTIMO ATO DA TRAGEDIA DANTESCA — Conduzido por companheiros de armas, êste soldado da Fôrça Pública de São Paulo deixa a Ilha para ser sepultado em Ubatuba, juntamente com as demais vítimas da evasão sem precedentes na historia penitenciaria mundial.

DE VOLTA AO XADREZ do Presídio, depois de ver frustrados os seus anseios de liberdade. Fracassou na tentativa doida de fugir.

Island Anchieta - Rebellion, the Truth and the Legends

PELAS PICADAS, os soldados da Força Pública adentravam as florestas da Serra do Mar. Muitas exageraram a autoridade. Outros cumpriram o dever.

A BUSCA DOS FORAGIDOS era efetuada em todos os recantos. Tudo foi vasculhado, sem grandes resultados. Os presos recapturados, em geral, renderam-se.

POR DETRÁS DAS ÁRVORES ou dos moitas poriam ser encontrados evadidos. Dos recapturados, maioria rendeu-se espontâneamente. Não resistiu

AINDA EM ESTADO DE CHOQUE, êste soldado foi encontrado vinte e quatro horas depois de ferido pelos presos.

te", do Presídio, que tem capacidade para umas cinquenta ou sessenta pessoas, um dos detentos que se recusou a fugir — Faria Júnior, condenado a 43 anos, 17 dos quais já cumpriu — ofereceu-se ao Diretor para combater.

— Tenha confiança em nós, Capitão. Somos mais de duzentos, fiéis à administração. Dê-nos armas que impediremos a fuga dos outros.

Consultando o Ten. Oduvaldo Silva, Comandante do destacamento militar da Ilha, resolveram ambos aceitar o oferecimento de Faria Júnior. Uns 60 presos foram armados e o tiroteio recomeçou. Os fugitivos já se encontravam na praia, a maioria inteiramente nua, Pereira Lima vestido de Tenente. Com as balas silvando ao seu redor, a situação para tomar a lancha chegou ao auge. A disputa por um lugar era realmente dramática. Muitos — segundo os depoimentos do Diretor Sadi Ferreira — se mataram nessa ocasião. Mas assim mesmo, fugindo para ou-

tros recantos da própria Ilha ou lançando-se ao mar com canoas e rebocavas, cerca de duzentos e trinta conseguiram evadir. Eram 14 horas de sexta-feira. Calcula-se que duas dezenas dos amotinados tenha morrido no tiroteio contra os fiéis às autoridades e que outro tanto tenha sido abatido pelos próprios companheiros, ou atropelo da fuga. O próprio Pereira Lima foi atingido por um tiro na testa, de raspão. Abolatados nas embarcações, dirigiram-se os fugitivos para a Enseada, para Ubatuba e para Ubatumirim daqui pegando rumo ao litoral norte, com intenção de atingir Cunha e Paratí, de onde ganhariam o interior do Estado de São Paulo e do Estado do Rio. Nos seus planos estavam incluídas operações militares em Enseada e Ubatuba, que seriam tomadas d'assalto e onde, cortadas tôdas as ligações com Santos e São Paulo, conseguiriam roupas para completar a evasão.

(CONCLUI NA PÁGINA 24)

A CADEIA DE PARATÍ há vários anos não abrigava nenhum prisioneiro. A pacata cidade do Estado do Rio esteve um polvorosa com o aparato policial na recaptura dos presidiários fugitivos. Aqui vemos quatro perigosos elementos presos com cautinosa à vista, nas últimas batidas feitas pela polícia nos matos circunvizinhos

O CRUZEIRO

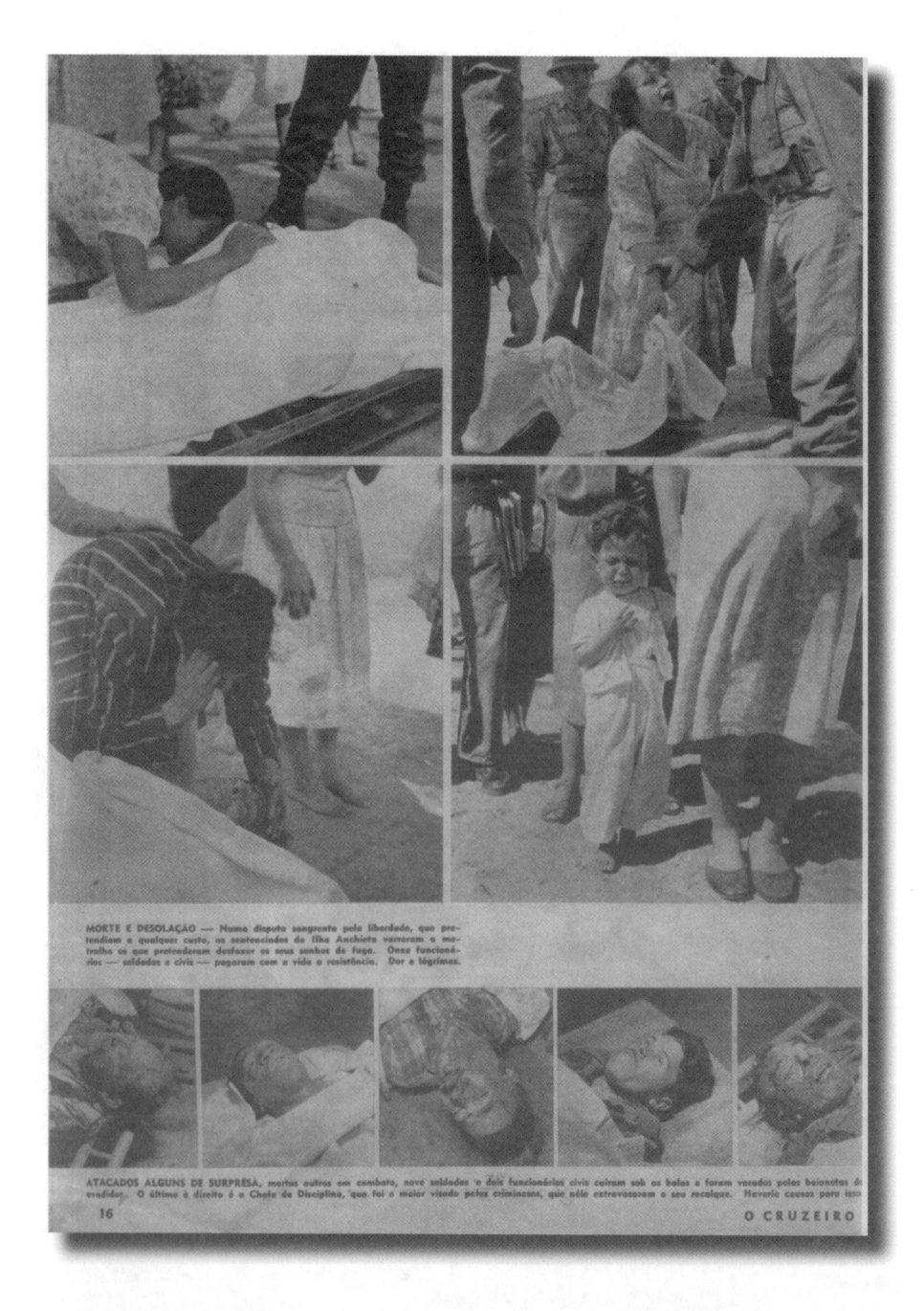

52   *Island Anchieta - Rebellion, the Truth and the Legends*

Island Anchieta - Rebellion, the Truth and the Legends

ÓDIO, LÁGRIMAS E LUTO NA

O PREÇO DA VINGANÇA

A RENDIÇÃO DO
CONDENADO

A PERSEGUIÇÃO NO MAR

A POLÍCIA MARÍTIMA DE SANTOS, utilizando-se de lanchas, patrulhava a costa, pronta para qualquer emergência. Varreu as praias que vão de Caraguatatuba a Ubatumirim. Posteriormente transportaram-se para Parati, a fim de auxiliar a caça que se fazia ao bando de Pereira Lima, acuado na serra.

CONDUZIDO A UBATUBA, ATIRADO À TERRA, nada mais restava para fazer. Além da gravidade do ferimento, haviam lhe dado água, o que determinou a sua morte. Examinado pelo médico do 5.º B. C., foi apenas constatado que já era um cadáver. Nenhum sentenciado, aliás, recebeu tratamento médico adequado.

5 de Julho de 1952 21

The Island in presente

First excursion in 1998 "inuite"

From left to right: Sergeant Laudelino, Dr^a Mara and Lieutenant Samuel. (1998)

From left to right: Sd. Afonso, Sgt. Afonso, Sgt. Montemor, Sub. Ten. Vilalba, Rosa and Sgt. Claudemir carrying his daughter Mariana. (1998)

Sapateiro Beach. (1998)

Sgt. João (left) and Sub-Lieutenant Clodomiro, having a snack on the island. (1998)

Lieutenant Costa (standing) and Lieutenant Guimarães. (1998)

Ariving at the island by schooner. (1998)

Dr^a. Mara, Sgt. Nanci and Sd. Afonso. (1998)

During the embarkation onto the schooner anchored in Saco da Ribeira, on the mainland, the Sub-Lieutenant and Sergeant (Regional de Taubaté), checking the passenger list. (1998)

Mass with the survivors of the upring on Ilha Anchieta.

Ruins of the prison. (1998)

From left to right: Milton Vieira, presidente dos Cabos e Soldados; Sub-Lieutenant Sodré, presidente dos Sub-Lieutenant e Sargentos; Cap. Palma (deceased) ex-presidente dos Oficiais da Reserva, reunidos com o Ten. Cel. Paulo Máximo, Cmt. do 5º BPMI. (1998)

From left to right: . Cel. Paulo Máximo, Dona Aydêe Cardoso and the ex-vice president of the reservists, Lieutenant Lázaro (deceased). (1998)

III - The truth and the legends

The island midwife
por Gracia Aparecida Prado Palma, filha da senhora Ana Rosa e do Soldado João Caetano de Olliveira

My father, Joao Caetano de Oliveira, who was a soldier in the military police, was ordered to go to work on Ilha Anchieta and, like any good father, took his family with him.

Shortly after we arrived, the wife of Private Misael, Senhora Antonia, was about to give birth. The midwife who lived in Saco da Ribeira (on the mainland) was called but the sea was too rough. Private Misael became very agitated and asked if anyone could help. My father took the liberty to offer the services of my mother and so the first baby she had ever delivered was born. My mother continued to help Senhora Antonia for forty days, as the custom then was that new mothers should not do any work for forty days, and should be fed only very bland chicken soup. What good times those were!

From then on, my mother delivered many babies. I don't remember the names of the children but I do remember some of the mothers names: Maria do Mangueirão; senhora Irene Soldier Lucas´s wife, senhora Jair Sargent Angelo Geraldo´s wife; senhora Mercedes Soldier Farias´s wife; senhora Cida Soldier Damasceno´s wife; senhora Nair Corporal Sudario´s wife; senhora Cida Soldier Meltíades´s wife; senhora Cida Soldier Araújo´s wife; senhora Maria Soldier José Alves´s wife. A senhora Maria, Mr Asterias' wife, had twins. The father of the twins was a civil servant working at the prison, as were the husbands of Senhora Olivia and Senhora Luzia. These are the only births I remember but there were many more.

The only complicated birth was that of Senhora Cecilia, Private Nelson Pintado's wife, which was a breach birth. Lieutenant Paulo was called upon to help. This must be why he says in his book that he was the "midwife" of the island. After the mutiny he returned to the island. If any children were born after 1952, then, yes, he was the one who delivered them but my mother was the midwife from April 1949 to April 1952.

The pearl of the northern São Paulo coast.
by Captain Res. Wilson Prado Palma

The pearl of the coast can be found in the Ubatuba district. Wonderful, beautiful, majestic, welcoming and full of history. I am, of course, referring to the Ilha Anchieta. At the present time each visitor to the island is charged two reais, to help cover the costs of making the island fit for tourism. With this money, the island authorities provide deckchairs and on the beach, four showers, drinking water and electric light. There is also a small boat which can be used to take tourists to the mainland if there is a medical emergency or some other urgent business. There are also trained guides to lead tourists along the rough paths on the island.

It is therefore obvious that a relaxing treasure like this needs a certain amount of cash to cover expenses. A large part of the money collected from the visitors goes on refuse collection as waste can be neither incinerated nor buried on the island as these damage the natural environment. For this reason, the rubbish is collected and transported to the mainland. The state does not have specific funds for this kind of service and so it is only right that the tourists should pay to keep the island unpolluted and to improve the facilities offered.

Ubatuba should be congratulated; it has become one of the unmissable parts of Brazil, for the beauty of its forests, crystalline waters, fantastic beaches, clean air and, above all, the historic nature of the Prison of Anchieta., a project first thought of in 1908 by Ramos de Azevedo during the government of Jorge Tibirica.

Unmissable because of the rebellion which broke out in the prison on the 20th June 1952, and because of the acts of the cacique Cunhambebe and Padre Anchieta, all events which are important to pass on to future generations.

Congratulations too to Parque Estadual da Ilha Anchieta, ao Engenheiro Dr. Manoel de Azevedo Fontes e á Bióloga Dr^a. Maria de Jesus Robim, responsável pelo Programa de Visitação Pública e Educação Ambiental da Ilha Anchieta.

This is the conclusion reached by the Commission Pro-Resgate Historico da Ilha Anchieta.

Boqueirão
by Captain Res. Wilson Prado Palma

Boqueirao is the part of the island which is closest to the mainland. The crossing here is about 600 metres wide and 38 to 42 metres deep.

The sea here can be turbulent, especially when an east wind is blowing but, when it isn't, the sea is very calm, with no big waves. In times gone by there were many big fish in these waters, indeed the Ilha was famous for its waters rich in fish. But much has changed.

After they began to use trawlers to fish, the shoals of fish were decimated. Trawlers, with their sonar radar and other modern equipment are able to find the fish easily. They can locate the shoals of fish in the distance and know how many fish there are and even what species. As the trawlers usually work in pairs, they string up the nets between the two boats and catch everything that moves! "Praise modernisation, death to nature".

At the time of the rebellion, on the other hand, there were lots of really big fish and one of the best known was the "tintureira". This was a kind of shark, really feared around those parts. It had an enormous mouth and extremely sharp teeth. They could snap in two sticks of wood six inches thick with a single bite. Several small fishing boats had been destroyed by these sharks; at least this is what the old-timers say.
The prisoners were afraid of the crossing. When the sea was calm the fishermen and the people who lived on the island would cross in rowing boats. Nowadays it is very uncommon for sharks, especially the dangerous types, to come into those waters. (*)

(*) N.A. Em 2003 aconteceram três casos: o primeiro tubarão ficou preso nas redes de pescadores no Boqueirão, o segundo foi morto a pauladas e cortado pelos caiçaras pescadores

na Praia da Enseada e o terceiro foi morto a pauladas pelos banhistas na Praia de Itamambuca.

The Mermaid of Ubatuba
by the author

When am I on the island, I allow myself to soar up on the wings of my imagination, and pass over forests, hilltops, rocks and beautiful beaches... I always end up thinking about the shortness of our time on this earth...

How many important people have deluded themselves, believing themselves to be eternal... but they are always betrayed by this body which withers away...

Sometimes power destroys our sense of reality. It makes us forget the fundamental law of our existence on earth, "dust to dust". I too believe in eternity... but of the spirit...

Seeing the beauty of the island, I notice that despite all the dreams of the various leaders who lived there, who felt themselves to be "owners" of the island ....they have all disappeared and only she, Anchieta, remains. They are history.

Beautiful Anchieta, your future "owners" will no doubt have similar dreams, but if each one mirrors the ones who have gone before, they will know that the queen is you... that you continue, down the years, to enchant unsuspecting sailors with your mermaid's arts...

Your charms can be transformed into sweet poison which leads your vain masters to taste agony, guilt and oblivion...

Speaking of this, we must remember the greatest of all the leaders who passed through, the great Cunhambebe, outstanding leader of the Tupinambas, who brought together the warriors of his Tamoio people, when Father Anchieta and Manoel de Nobrega were alive, and who liberated the native Indians from Portuguese slavery and collaborated in expelling the French from Brazilian soil, at the time when Anchieta was a hostage of the Tupinambas in Iperoig (now Ubatuba).

Cunhambepe was the first to think he owned the "Mermaid". He negotiated peace between the Portuguese and the indigenous peoples on this strip of coast in the second half of the sixteenth century.

Schooners anchored off the island. (1998)

My return to the island after 46 years
by Gracia Aparecida Prado Palma

After a gap of 46 years, thanks to God (and to my friends) I was given the opportunity to spend two days on the island. It was wonderful chance to reflect and to remember. I felt at home again. I went back to see all the places I used to know. I returned to the old "Vila Militar" even though hardly anything of it remained. You couldn't even call what was left of it "ruins", as absolutely nothing was left, apart from foundations of the houses. The only two houses standing were two that had been built after the rebellion, after I'd left.

The barracks was still standing, but it will soon collapse if nothing is done to look after it. We looked for, and found, the old cemetery, by now grown over with weeds. I had only been there three times before; for the funerals of two children and a prisoner. I also went to Praia Grande (as it was called), and Prainha (little beach) and to Pocinho, where my father had taught me how to swim.

I remembered my parents and my three sisters, Lazara, Aparecida and Maria. I had a vivid memory of my mother on the small beach, stick in hand, calling out that we were not too go too far into the sea, that the waves could be treacherous. I remembered all the picnics we'd had on Praia do Sul (south beach), having a great time with my parents and my friends, never overshadowed by the dangers of the place.

The night of my return visit, we stayed up late talking. Even I after I went to bed, I wasn't able to sleep; alongside the euphoria of being back on the island, were my memories of everything and of everybody. Oh, how well I remembered the teacher, Dona Mercedes. She was a wonderful person. I thought about all my little schoolfriends, and remembered each one, what they used to like, what they used to do at break time. I will never forget how I felt that night lying awake in on the island, surrounded by my memories. In the morning I walked along the road which used to lead to the school. Now there is a little hotel there instead.

I also remembered the Sunday visits to Dona Antonia's house. While we children used to play, she and my mother used to make little corn cakes to have with coffee in the afternoon.

I remembered all those who had died on that fateful day of the rebellion; I had known them all. I felt sorry for their children. They were my friends. So much pain, so much sadness. I had never ever spoken to them about what had happened that day; I had never been brave enough. I lost my own father years later in a car accident, so I know what sadness is.

I would like to spend more time on Ilha Anchieta to remember all those things we used to do which made an impression on me; the Christmas parties, the country dances which were held in the hospital block, the barbeques which the Prison Director would organise for his friends, and to which nearly all the families went, including mine. After a gap of 46 years, it was a wonderful experience to set foot on Ilha Anchieta again and to feel such nostalgia, sadness and happiness all mixed up.

In the front row from left to right, Sra. Sônia, wife of Coronel EB Albano, ex-Comandante of 2° BECmb, the Colonel himself and the teacher Mérica, ex-vice Prefeita de Taubaté.

Politicians, civil, militaty authorities and the president of these associations at the mass with the children of the island (1999). Seated in the centre are Milton vieira and the Capitain Palma (deceased)

Lenina, adviser to the mayor of Ubatuba, radio announcer Jura Belo, Dr^a. Mara, Dr. Airton Barbosa and his son filho Everton.

Pô-Quá
by the author

I have heard several people say that the reason Ilha anchieta was called Ilha dos Porcos (island of pigs) was because the inhabitants used to raise pigs, and, after killing them to eat, would throw all the parts they didn't want into the Boqueirao in order to attract sharks, thus making it more difficult for the prisoners to escape by swimming.

It's a lovely story, but has no truth to it unfortunately, as I will try to show.

It is true that there were sharks in these waters from at least the beginning of the twentieth century, but the name Ilha dos Porcos comes from much earlier, from the seventeenth century in fact. It was a corruption of the Tupi (indigenous) word, Po-Qua, meaning pointed; pointed, because of the two hills, one at either end of the island, the Morro de Papagaio and the Morro do Farol. It was an easy step from Pô-Quá to "Porco"!

In the old seventeenth century archives dealing with division of land, (long before a prison on the island had been planned) the island was called "Ilha Dos Porcos". This shows that the "to feed the sharks" explanation, is not the right one, since the prison was only opened in 1908, three hundred years later!

On 19th March 1934, the island's official name was changed to Ilha Anchieta, to mark the 400th anniversary of Padre José de Anchieta's birth.

The original name of the island was Tapera or Terra de Cunhambepe, the most famous of the caciques of the Tupinamba tribe who were the first people to live there. Indeed, they were often called "Tamoios", which means "first inhabitants".

Author's note: There is a story that, on the day of the rebellion, the soldier who used to feed the sharks with the odds and ends of the pigs was swimming across to the mainland when he was surrounded by these savages of the sea. He raised himself out of the water so they could see him properly. This they did and let him through...
This is obviously not even a myth; just a joke!

I saw the rebellion
by Zenaide

My name is Zenaide de Oliveira Franco Dos Santos. I am the daughter of Captain of the Reserves, the late Cherubim de Lima Franco, who was a sergeant at the time of the rebellion, and his wife, Senhora Francisca Oliveira Franco.

We used to live in the Vila Militar of Ilha Anchieta, the first house on the left after the Military Detachment.

We lived next door to Private Otavio dos Santos, his wife Dona Benedita and their seven or eight children.

When the rebellion took place, the day was cold and dark, like it is when there's an eclipse of the sun.

I was thirteen at the time and was in the back yard, pouring water into dishes for the ducks which we used to keep. Over the top of the bamboo fence looking on to the Detachment, I suddenly caught sight of a soldier running towards our back yard. He was caught by a group of prisoners and beaten to death with a stick. I stood frozen to the spot, not hearing the frantic cries of my mother telling me to come into the house. Just then I heard a shot from within the barracks and Dona Benedita's voice screaming "Oh, my Octavio!". Her husband had been shot dead.

At this point I managed to run to my mother and, together with my sister Zelia, we lay down on the floor, where we stayed till the shoot-out was over.

The prisoners arrived later on and rounded up several families and took us all to the milking sheds. On the way there one of the prisoners began to touch one of our neighbours, a pretty young girl.....the rebel leader, Joao Pereira Lima, aimed at the ground and fired right by the prisoner's foot and said:

- "Whoever messes with women or children will be killed by me personally. Never forget, our aim is just to escape!".

My mother wrapped up my father's ammunition in a pillow and carried it out with her.

One of the prisoners asked her what she had with her and she replied that it was my little brother's special pillow, the one he always used in order to get to sleep.

From the milking shed we were taken to the prison and locked up in one of the wings. We had to wait till the next day to be let out.

My father wasn't on the island as he had travelled to Taubate.

We hadn't been able to find my little brother that day and he was lost to us but the next day we found him, safe and sound, luckily.

Dr Colonel Moacyr Hoelz
by the author

In 1952, the doctor working in the 5th battalion in Taubate was a person who had dedicated his life to helping those who needed his services, whether rich or poor.

Whenever a doctor was needed, there was the beloved Dr Moacyr Hoelz.

He loved the Military Police with the devotion of one who has found his calling, and he didn't hesitate to give any assistance he could to the sick, the injured and the anguished. He was adored by the troops, his friends and family until the end of his life; indeed, he is still loved by them as can be seen by their words whenever his name is mentioned.

At the time of the rebellion, he went straight there to try and save the lives of the many injured. He stayed there for five days, until he had done everything humanly possible to help.

He was criticised by the tabloid press who wanted to see him brought to his knees by the unenviable choice he faced as to whether to treat the injured rebels or the police but he didn't bat an eyelid; he treated both.

He died 10 years ago leaving a wife and children, sad but proud of their husband, father, doctor and military man they had in their family.

May he be in God's good care.

The Day of the Rebellion
by Rita

Dona Rita Maria da Cruz was married to the civil servant, Francisco Silva Cruz, one of the prison guards. They were married in a civil ceremony in Ubatuba on 27th January 1940 and had the religious blessing in the little chapel of Senhor Bom Jesus later that same year.

They had four children; Edneia, Sidneia, Dioneaia and Lucineia. They had lived on the island for 12 years when the rebellion took place...

Francisco had the night before the rebellion off. He had worked until late and, after handing over to a colleague he went to his house in Praia Grande and slept till the morning. When the sun was already high in the sky, he went towards the Administration block to take the girl who worked for them to see the dentist.

On the way there, near the prison, he heard machine-gun fire and saw bullets whizzing into the trees. He decided to leave the dentist for another day, and went instead to the school to collect his two daughters Edneia and Dioneaia and took them home. On the way, he got six more children whose parents weren't at home and took them with him.

Straight after they got home, two prisoners appeared and one of them begged him to flee his house with the children, for the love of God, as "Barranquinha" was looking for him in order to kill him as he had sworn he would do one day.

Francisco took his wife, children, the maid and the six other children and they left by the back and went to hide in Praia de Sul where he knew of a good hiding place amongst the vegetation which he had used many times when hunting.

When Barranquinha arrived at the house, he was stopped by the prisoners loyal to Francisco, and, finding his way barred, he gave up on the idea of murder and decide to leave the island as quickly as he could along with the other mutineers who were leaving for the mainland in boats.

At about 4 pm, Francisco was found by Asterio, one of the civilian workers who also knew of the hiding place, and, accompanied by one of the soldiers, they all went to one of the wings of the prison where they stayed

till the early hours when reinforcements arrived from Taubate.
Dona Rita is Henrique's godmother, the boy who was born that night inside the prison and who is now 47 and works for Ford in Taubate.
Francisco died more than five years ago.
His wife still lives in Ubatuba and is now more than seventy and his daughters are both in their fifties.

I was married and just 17 years old
by Maria Aydêe Cardoso

46° aniversário da Rebelião da Ilha Anchieta Comemorações e Reencontros

The 20th June 1998. That day, exactly 46 years after the rebellion, the event was commemorated and we met up again with several people who had been on the island at the time of the famous rebellion.

The acts of commemoration took place in the Barracks of the 5° B.C. (today 5° BPMI in Taubaté) under the command of Colonel Paulo Máximo.

A mass was celebrated at nine o'clock that morning in memory of the soldiers and workers who had shed their blood in the line of duty. Father Fred, the vicar of the parish of São José Operário, celebrated the Mass, helped by Senhora Magdalena. The mass was made even more beautiful by the singing of a wonderful choir. The consecration of the bread and wine were very special moments for me, as Father Fred read out the names of all those who had died...

After the religious ceremony there was a military procession with soldiers of both sexes. The special edition of "Noticias Policias" was given to all those present, with a long article about and many photos of the rebellion. Colonel Nelson Francisco Duarte, Colonel Paulo Cesar Máximo and all the members of the Commission Pró Rescue Historical of the Ilha Anchieta they were present.

The commemoration finished with a delicious lunch in the battalion. A diploma was given by the Commission to all those who had been present on the island that tragic day. The following day, 21st June

1998, as part of the commemoration, the organising committee had organised a trip to the island and we left at 7am from Taubaté in a bus of the ERT. We were escorted all the way by two vehicles, one belonging to the PM and the other belonging to the Transport police.

There was only one topic on everybody's lips; the Ilha Anchieta rebellion.

Those who had never been to Anchieta, were very eager to see the place they had heard so much about, and those of us returning were excited too. We went from the mainland to the island by schooner.

Luckily, the sea was calm that day. A light breeze was blowing from the north and seagulls flew over the boat as we made our way to the island. I felt very strange; I can't really explain, as if my heart were aching... it was a very emotional moment for me.

When we were still about 250 metres from where we were going to disembark, Eduardo Sene, a military man, who had been on the island at the time of the rebellion, looked at a stretch of coast and said to José Chagas:

- "Do you remember how Simao had to walk a long way to get to that coast?"

When the soldiers first found out about the revolt, before the reinforcements had arrived, they decided to go to the island and caught sight of Simao. Thinking he was one of the prisoners, they shot at him, but luckily he wasn't hit.

- "They were afraid to disembark and turned back..."
- "Simao swam more than a kilometre across the Boqueirao in order to tell Afonso, who was on duty on the other side, on the mainland. He was in a sentry tower, which was little more than a hut with a thatched roof, which was used as a look-out. The boatmen used to take him lunch and snacks whenever he was on duty".

Afonso was told and managed to let the Fifth Battalion of (Caçadores) know.

Returning to our trip 46 years later, once our schooner had arrived at Anchieta, we had to wait for two hours to disembark. This was because we did not have the right papers giving us permission and the person in charge couldn't be found. Building work was being done. At last, Lieutenant Colonel Paulo Cesar Maximo, President of the Commission, was found and after a long conversation we were allowed to disembark and we went to the prison. It was just like a movie for me.

Straight after we were married, Walter, my husband, Corporal in the Military Police, was chosen to work in the prison on Ilha Anchieta. That same prison, which had so many infamous prisoners behind its bars, is nowadays in ruins and in a state of utter neglect.

When I arrived to live on the island I quickly made friends with the other wives there. I wanted to find out all I could about the island; it was all very strange for me.

The first thing I heard didn't please me at all, in fact, it terrified me. The prisoners had been given orders to work in the soldiers' houses, where they cleared vegetable patches, made fences and chopped wood.

I was told that a year before, Pereira Lima, along with some others, had made a canoe and oars in order to escape the island, but that it hadn't worked out. "Portugal Pacheco", the head of Discipline had got to hear of it and had gone out with an escort, and made PL and the others carry the canoe on their shoulders as far as the prison. As they passed through the Vila Militar, he began to hit PL around the face with one of the oars. The boat was heavy, PL was sweating, his shoulders were bleeding and some of the women cried at the sight of this.

The team of Portugal Pacheco was composed of The team of Portugal Pacheco was composed of Sargent Cherubim, Corporal Sudario and Soldiers Nelson de Jesus and Damásio.

My husband wasn't pleased to hear all this but he said that women always exaggerated and that I shouldn't talk to them about these things or I would get upset.

As time passed, I realised that the "hell-hole" I found myself in wasn't as bad as it had seemed at first sight.

Obviously I owed a lot to my dear, now departed husband. He did everything he could to help me get used to the place, where the only form of entertainment was having picnics on the beach.

One day he said to me, "I'm going to take you to a really pretty place. It's called Saco Grande".

On his day off we went; we took binoculars with us. It was pure scrubland there, a rocky hill about 50 metres high with a beautiful view and huge turtles.

A local man told me that if you managed to catch one of the turtles and removed its shell, it would be big enough to have baths in!

I saw many different things.

The prisoners were always distributing notes saying there was going to be a rebellion, but no-one believed them...

On the 20th June 1952, a group of 117 prisoners went to look for wood.

At nine o'clock, I leaned out of the window of our house in the Vila military, when I saw them pass, each one had a log of wood on his shoulders and the two at the front were armed. Surprised, I said to my neighbour, Private Laurindo's wife, "The group are back really early today, Dona Ester!".

At that very moment, I heard a loud shot from the direction of the barracks; I later learned that it was the shot which killed Private Otavio, the gunsmith.

When I looked round, I saw Dona Nair, Private Lucas's wife, shouting to me in desperation, and behind her, two men, armed and covered in blood, asking "Where is your husband?".

My voice failed me and they shouted again, "Where's your husband?".

I said, "He's at the barracks" .

I jumped out of the window. There were some steps down to the road. I saw some prisoners huddled together under the steps and heard many shots. I crossed the road to Dona Nair's house.

I also saw Dona Irene, Lucas's wife. He went out of the house with an axe to confront a group of four prisoners but they grabbed hold of the axe and split his head open with one blow.

We stayed in Dona Nair's house, with Dona Ester, a four-month old baby and a three-year old child, Dona Mercedes and Faria's children.

We said many prayers, and looked through the gap in the window and saw prisoners running and swearing as they ran.

They took off all the boats and canoes that they could lay their hands on. There was a boat called "Maracana" which the soldiers had bought for 400,000 reais for the use of the families.

After a few minutes there was a knock on the door. There were six prisoners outside. We were terrified but they said that they came as friends and that if we didn't open up they would knock down the door.

We opened the door and fell down on our knees and begged them not to do anything to us.

They told us they were taking us to a place where we would be safe.

We went out one after the other, as if in a procession, and went to the house of the milkman, Geraldo Antunes, who raised pigs. His was the last house, right out into the countryside, with five small rooms.

We all stayed there as long as they wanted us to.

At 5pm, they released Lieutenant Odvaldo from his cell. The prison director, Sadi, and his family were let out, as well as the doctor. Accompanied by a few of the prisoners they came to look for us in Geraldo Nunes' house and they took us to the prison to be with the others. I carried Dona Ester's four-month old baby and she carried the three-year old child. When we walked past the barracks we saw a lot of blood and she recognised Laurindo's handkerchief. She became hysterical and at that point we all began to cry.

As we drew close to the prison I saw Dona Maria, wife of the civil servant, Irineu. She was crying and holding her stomach; she was expecting a baby. She and Dona Aurelia went into one of the cells and, six hours later, at 11pm, a baby was born. They called him Henrique Antonio de Oliveira. Dona Aurelia acted as midwife.

That night, at around 8pm, my husband Walter appeared, limping and without his cap. When I caught sight of him we fell into each other's arms and he, with great concern, asked me if the prisoners had done anything to us.

I cried with happiness to see him and, at the same time, with despair.

At around 6am reinforcements came to take back the island. PM (Força Pública), Army and Sea Police.

When Doctor Moacyr and Colonel Hidalgo came into the prison with caps under their arms, the women who had lost their husbands rushed forward to embrace them as if they were their fathers. We all cried.

I also remember that there was one soldier, Marcelino, but called "Boiadeiro" by everyone, who fled the barracks at the moment of the rebellion and fell into a deep hole. He was only found five days later. A stretcher was made from wood and they took him to the makeshift hospital where he was tended to by Dr Funcio, put on a drip and given light food until he was well again.

The first house we were given when we went to live on the island had three rooms, a big table and a bench in the sitting room. We had to cook on a wood-burning stove but we did have a little paraffin stove for when we wanted to make a quick coffee. We did have a shower, thank God. We brought our own bed.

Before the rebellion, they put on a play about Christ's crucifixion and performed it in the streets. The principal role was played by a soldier called Joao Alves, known by the name Santo Cristo. It was a lovely piece of theatre.

I also recall that Private Afonso was very religious. He prayed and said the rosary every Sunday and we all sang hymns together.
I still remember Dona Ana, wife of Private João Caetano (who was well known in Pindamonhangaba) and who lived on the island until March 1952, four months before the rebellion. She was a very good midwife, much sought after, and she used to take her two little girls, Maria and Gracia, along with her whenever she was called to help deliver a baby, so that they could play with the other children in the mother-to-be's house, if there were any.

Gracia is now a widow; her husband was Captain Palma, and Maria is my brother's wife, Sergeant Paulo Salgado.

Dona Ana would always take the mother's and baby's clothes to her own house to wash. She would say how she liked to help people when they most needed it.

Captain Paulo Vianna lived on the island on two occasions, before and then again after the rebellion.

He and his wife, Dona Gineta, would also deliver babies when there was no-one else to do it. Before the rebellion PV had liked to take prisoners home with him on special occasions like birthdays or at carnival to play the guitar, tambourine or drums. At 11pm the prisoner would be picked up and taken back to the prison.

The second time that PV lived on the island, I became very friendly with his wife, Dona Gineta. We would go to the beach together, taking the children, Dede, Paulinho and her little girl, Marta. It was she who taught me how to float face down in the water.

It seems like yesterday; I remember that Portugal Pacheco's wife was called Dona Odete. She was a lovely lady, tall, blond, blue-eyed, who wore her hair to one side. On the day of the rebellion her husband was killed right in front of her and their younger children. The other two children were at school.

The day after the rebellion, a helicopter landed on Praia Grande and took away the teacher, Mercedes. When the prisoners were being beaten on the beach nearest the school, she would close the book and say, "the lesson's over, let's all sing now", so that the children wouldn't hear the moans of the prisoners or the noise of the beatings.

In the evenings we would go to Lieutenant Odvaldo's house. His wife, Zuleica, used to make little cakes and tell stories. When we returned to live in Taubate, I was already expecting our son, Waltinho.

When I thought that the things that had happened on Anchieta were safely behind us, something new emerged. In April 1953, nearly a year after the rebellion, my husband Walter was working in a police station in Sao Paulo and we were living in Taubate. Waltinho was just two weeks old, when I began to get worried because my husband hadn't come home after work like he usually did. Then my late brother Guido came over with a newspaper from the capital, Sao Paulo, the headline of which read, "Soldiers responsible for Ilha Anchieta rebellion taken prisoner". My husband, along with other soldiers, remained in the military prison Romao Gomes, in Barro Branco, Sao Paulo, from April to September 1953. Five and a half months that I had to go and work to support myself and my little son so that we wouldn't go hungry...

At this point I would like to express my gratitude to my parents, who have now passed away, for helping me at that difficult time.

Thank you, father, Abilio, thank you mother, Vitoria.

The soldiers who were imprisoned in military prison Romão Gomes were Corporal Walter Cardoso, Soldiers: Darci Vargas, Eduardo Sene, José Chagas, José Maria, Benedito dos Santos e José Marcelino.

Lieutenant Odvaldo was also punished, not by being imprisoned in Romão Gomes, but by being forbidden to carry out his duties for a certain period of time.

After five and a half months they were acquitted and released but we never got a penny in compensation.

On my return to the island in 1998, what really moved me was being able to put flowers on the memorial to PM Laurindo, in front of the barracks, where I had suffered so much.

One day, Lieutenant Samuel and his wife, Dr Mara, happened to go to Pouso Frio and passed by my son Waltinho's farm, Sitio Bom Jesus. They met him and exchanged ideas. The topic of Ilha Anchieta came up. I got to know them later. We had long conversations and the idea of this commemoration came about, this wonderful event of 20th and 21st June 1998, which made me remember and write down what happened for my children and grandchildren.

Thank you, Lieutenant Samuel and Dr Mara for giving me this opportunity.

*Some children residents of
the island in 1951*

*Retired Sergeant Afonso Alves in the day of the rebellion was of service in
the Position of Epia. (1998)*

Lieutenant Faria
by the author

Lieutenant Milton Fernandes de Faria, nowadays in the Reserve of the Military Police, can often be seen at the Association for reserve PM officers in Taubate, where he meets up with friends and colleagues to pass the time.

It was on one of his visits there that I met him and we talked about Ilha Anchieta. I could see he was getting very emotional talking about the rebellion. I first thought of trying to change the subject but then I realised it might be a good idea for him to unburden himself, that talking about it might be cathartic, something I had seen with other "Filhos da Ilha". So, I listened intently to what he had to say.

His eyes wet with tears, he recalled the morning of 20th June 1952. His father, Private Sebastiao Fernandes de Faria, known as "Sepultura" (Tomb), had returned home from working as a guard at the barracks. He said hello to Dona Mercedes, his wife, and to the young Milton and his two little daughters, Marlene and Marilene. He told them that he had handed over to Laurindo,(COMPADRE) the soldier who was now on guard duty.

Suddenly, a shot and a loud scream rang out.

His father told his mother that he would go and have a look to see what was happening. Milton accompanied him as far as the door and saw some prisoners throwing the bundles of wood that they had been carrying on their shoulders onto the ground. His father returned quickly telling them that the prisoners had taken over the Detachment. He gave orders to his wife to leave with the children, saying that he himself would go out through the back yard. Milton's mother and sisters left by the front door but Milton tried to follow his father, but it was too late; he had already disappeared. He ran towards the front of the house where his mother, by now in the street, was calling him, and he saw a prisoner, armed with a rifle, blocking the gate through which he had to pass. His mother begged, "Please let my son through!"

The prisoner replied:

"Don't worry. We won't hurt the families".

Milton went with his mother and sisters to Private Meltiades' house and there they locked themselves in with another family. Almost immediately a group of prisoners knocked on the door and ordered them all out, taking them to a cowshed near Saco Grande. On the way there they passed another group of prisoners who were coming in the opposite direction, Milton remembers how frightened he was and how he looked away, towards the river bank, rather then look them in the eyes. He heard the same prisoner as before say, "Relax, nothing bad is going to happen to you".

They stayed in the cowshed, where Geraldo Antunes used to work, until they were once again led away, this time to one of the wings of the prison, where they would spend the whole night, only being set free the next day when the reinforcements arrived and the situation was under control.

They went home. There they found everything upside down; even the hen's nest had been overturned and the vulture's eggs given to them by one of the prisoners and which his mother had put there to hatch, had been broken.

Their godfather Laurindo had been beaten to death.

When the prison was closed, his family left the island and went to live in Taubate. His father was transferred to to the 5th Batallion. In Taubate, three more little brothers and sisters were born – Jose Carlos, Sidney and Marineusa.

Lieutenant Faria is one of the "Filhos da Ilha" who was born on Anchieta and who now comes every single year to our annual events there.

Difficult moments
by Maria Galvão

Ilha Anchieta was really pretty, and it still has beautiful beaches...I had lived there since 1949. My husband was a nurse and worked in the pharmacy there. We had two daughters. When the rebellion began on 20th June 1952, he had already left for work. I was at home with my daughters and my mother-in-law. Senhor Marcondes, one of the prisoners, who worked for us in the house, was sweeping the back yard.

It was about eight o'clock in the morning when we heard a shot. Straight afterwards, we heard two more. Worried, I ran to the window because from there it was possible to see the barracks. The prisoner who was working for us, stopped and, when he saw me, said, "Go inside, Dona Maria, and shut all the windows because the prisoners have taken over the barracks. I closed the window. Just then my neighbour came over; she was terrified too. Senhor Marcondes wanted to come inside with us, he said he would protect us, but we were too frightened to let him. I didn't know if we could trust him; after all, he was a prisoner too. My neighbour and friend was Antonilha, now Sr Paulo's wife, who was a private at that time. She wanted us to go together to his house.

When we got there, we found two more friends there, Maria, the wife of one of the builders, Crespo, and Cacilda, Escoteiro's wife. Escoteiro was one of the civilian workers there. Their children were with them. We stayed there praying that it would all be over soon and that no-one would get hurt. We heard lots of shots and machine-gun fire; it sounded like a war was going on. At about 9.30am, Paulo came in to get more ammunition as his had run out. Paulo was the son of Sr Gabriel, the man who worked on the boat "Carneiro da Fonte", which was used to transport things between the island and the mainland. Antonilha tried to stop him leaving, but he rushed out, leaving his shirt in her hands. Bullets continued to whizz all around us. At 11am the boys went to the vegetable garden and were told that one of the nurses who worked in the pharmacy had been killed. I was terrified it was my husband, but they tried to reassure me by saying that it was sure to have been Sergeant Melchiades, who didn't have a very good relationship with some of the prisoners. Even so, I was still worried as I didn't know for sure what had happened.

At midday, the boat which sailed between Santos and Ubatuba, and which stopped off on the island to leave provisions and medicines, was coming in to moor on the island when the crew saw smoke....they were suspicious and decided not to moor but rather to return to Ubatuba and let the authorities know that something strange was going on. The prisoners had been waiting for the boat to moor as they, hidden in the undergrowth, were planning to take charge of the boat and escape in it but now this wasn't going to happen. They were furious, and threw themselves at the boat but to no avail. The rebels were now frightened as they knew that police reinforcements would soon arrive from the mainland. Some of the prisoners got hold of canoes and little boats and fled when they saw the big boat turn round. Those who stayed knew that more police would soon arrive and that there was no point in trying to escape. They went through the streets shouting that there were coming for the women and children. We panicked when we heard them as we had no idea what they would do to us.

We had left by the back of the house and had gone to Sr Eugenio's house, where his wife Geni was alone with their children, when some prisoners dressed in military uniforms arrived. Believing they had some of the island workers with them, we asked if we could go to Sr Geraldo's house, which was in the Vila Militar. When we got there, we heard more shots; it was now after 3pm. Everybody was rushing around in a panic. We all went into one of the rooms. We were terrified. Sr Geraldo made a white flag that we could wave as a sign of peace. Some prisoners arrived and told the women and children to go to the prison, where their husbands had been rounded up.

As we walked to the prison we saw the corpses of soldiers lying on the ground, provisions scattered around, smoke....a real horror! We got to the prison and saw some of the workers. My husband wasn't there, but Escoteiro told me to calm down, that it was Sergeant Melchiades who had been killed. We heard how, right at the beginning of the mutiny, the prisoners had caught hold of the doctor, Antonio Inocente Fonte, recently married, and who had only come to work on the island two months before.

The director and lieutenant Odvaldo had also been locked up, together with their wives, but they had now been set free. We stayed in the cells. We were offered food and were given mattresses so that we could lie down but no-one was hungry....My husband came to the cell, and it was only then that I believed he was alive. He returned to the pharmacy as there were many injured who needed his help. We stayed there and, towards morning, we heard shots and shouting again....The police reinforcements were arriving and some of the prisoners, who had hidden in the undergrowth, were firing at them. Suddenly, it was all over! The prisoners had surrendered. We stayed where we were until the following day; it was only then that we were able to go home. We found out that the people who worked on the boat, sr Antonio, sr Gabriel and Sr Eugenio, had been found, tied up, amongst the vegetation. The husband told me afterwards that the three leaders of the rebellion, all armed, had turned up at the pharmacy and had taken Sergeant Melchiades. They had said to my husband, "Senhor Romao, you stay here, d'you hear? You are going to have a lot of work today....the island belongs to us!

My husband begged them not to take the sergeant but they pretended not to hear. Later he learnt that they had killed him.

We stayed on the island for a further after three years after the rebellion, but some things changed. The prisoners continued to be let out of the prison to work, but fewer of them at a time, and the soldiers and prison guards became more careful....But the fear was always there; only those who were there on the island on that fateful day can judge how dangerous the situation had been for us.

Lieutenant Norival dos Santos
by the author

Lietenant Norival was second Sergeant of the Security Forces at the 5th Battalion on the day of the rebellion, 20th June 1952. He was returning to the barracks in Taubate for the afternoon shift, when he saw Colonel Hidalgo calling the soldiers together in the inside patio.

When they had been told what was going on, he and Sergeant Dorival Prado armed themselves. Dorival took a machine gun and Norival took a rifle and plenty of ammunition.

The situation had been assessed as being extremely serious and for this reason they were going out heavily armed, ready for whatever they might find.

The commander ordered a lorry to come to the front of the barracks.

He told them to fill up the tank and check the tyres. The load was checked and they were on their way to Ubatuba.

At the top of the mountain they got out of the lorry and walked down to the sea in groups of three. They arrived in the town of Ubatuba at about six o'clock. It was raining and was very cold.

Colonel Hidalgo got all his troops together in the central square and gave a platoon to Lieutenant Idalecio. They set off towards the Praia da Enseada, where they knew the boat "Ubatubinha" was anchored. This was the boat that the prisoners had been waiting for, but which had stayed moored in Ubatuba because of the bad weather forecast, and had not crossed that day (see more in the chapter, "Rebellion").

When the platoon led by Lieutenant Idalecio, which included the two sergeants Norival and Dorival, was getting close to the Praia das Toninhos, they caught sight of car headlights in the distance. The Lieutenant decided that the men should wait at the side of the road and that the last in line should intercept the convoy. The last man was Sergeant Norival.

He stood in the middle of the road and signalled to the convoy that it should stop. They saw who was in the group. It consisted of the police chief, Dr Centola, and several investigators from the capital, all heavily armed. The Lieutenant went to speak to the police chief and Sergeant Norival heard him say that he was taking his troops to Ilha Anchieta. The police chief replied that that was a crazy thing to do. The lieutenant confirmed that he had "his destination was the island and that was where he was going". The police chief replied, "that is crazy, lieutenant, all your troops will be killed".

But Lieutenant Idalecio had made up his mind and replied, "Then so be it, but go we must".

The police chief asked after the colonel and was told he was in Ubatuba. He set off with his men to see him.

The platoon continued walking towards the Praia de Enseada and saw the boat they were looking for in the distance out at sea. To reach it, they had to use a small boat which only took three people at a time. The journeys between the beach and the boat could only take place at the speed of the oar.

Sergeant Norival saw a fiery black stallion on the deck of the

Ubatubinha. It looked Arabic and was in a small, improvised pen. "We learned later that it was being sent out to the Director Sadi."

The deck of the boat was full of provisions which were due to have been unloaded on Ilha Anchieta the day of the rebellion.

There was a long delay while all the soldiers got on board, because of the slowness of the dinghy, as we have seen. When the last three were embarking, the police chief arrived with Colonel Hidalgo.

After these last two had embarked, they all set off for the island on "Ubatubinha". They arrived at around one thirty in the morning of the 21st June, with all the lights off. Once on the pier, Colonel Hidalgo shouted to Directo Sadi, who answered and approached the boat. When the Colonel asked him how he was, he answered, "Everything that had to happen has happened. You can disembark, it's OK now."

The troops disembarked, together with the civilian police and found the island under the command of the prisoner Faria Junior, who, dressed in uniform, had been the Acting Commander for several hours by this time. He had kept order, relying on men who were loyal to him, using force if necessary, preventing any maltreatment of the soldiers' and civilian officials' families. (You can read about Faria later on in the book). Norival and his colleagues stayed on the island until order had been completely restored.

The Funeral
by the author

He arrived on the Ilha Anchieta in the early hours of 21st June, together with the first group of police under the command of Colonel Hidalgo, and was there when they made contact with the group of prisoners led by Faria Junior. They set free the families who had been locked in cells for their own safety, and had been guarded by the prisoners who had remained loyal and not joined the rebellion.

Sergeant Jose Luiz stayed on the island for a week to make sure everything was put in order. His wife, Dona Amelia, stayed in Sao Jose dos Campos with their children Reynaldo, Pedro, Celia and Jose

Luiz, waiting for news of her husband, not knowing why he hadn't come home. The military culture in those days didn't worry about letting families know where their loved ones were and so they only got to know that Jose Luiz had been on the coast trying to re-capture the prisoners who had fled, when he returned home a week later.

When Sergeant Jose Luiz was on the island, one of his jobs was to arrange the funerals of the men who had died; one sergeant, one corporal, six soldiers and two civilians. Their bodies were taken to Ubatuba and they were buried in tombs in the graveyard so that the men who had died fighting for the island would always be remembered. As Lieutenant of the PM Reserve, Jose Luiz told us that hardly any family members made an appearance at the funeral, maybe because it was difficult for them to get transport, or maybe because of the horrible way in which their loved ones had died.

Lieutenant Jose Luiz has now passed away, but he left eight children, four sons and four daughters; those which have already been mentioned and those who were born after his return from the island – Carlos, Silvia, Cristina and Rita. When I interviewed him, he was quite advanced in years but his mind was still sharp and he still got upset when he remembered what he had seen on that terrible trip.

P.S. O cemitério onde estão os ossos dos falecidos é o Cemitério Central, antigo de Santa Cruz, de Ubatuba.

The "Scout"
by the author

(One afternoon I was in the rooms belonging to the association of the Officials of the Reservation in the city of Taubaté) when a gentleman of about seventy approached me; I would later find out that he was, in fact, nearly eighty, of medium height, stocky, bright-eyed and firm on his feet. He asked me if I was Lieutenant Samuel, and when I replied that I was he continued, "Is it true that you are making an excursion to Ilha Anchieta on 20th June, and taking the survivors of the rebellion, the so-called 'Filhos de Ilha'?".

I had hardly finished replying that yes, it was true, when he started speaking again, more anxiously this time.

"Well, I am a "Filho da Ilha". I lived there for many years, and I was on the mainland with a group of soldiers under the command of a corporal when the mutiny occurred. We had been there since the night before on the orders of a Lieutenant, commander of the Military guard, to look for a prisoner called "Dentinho" who had been killed and buried on the Praia das Palmas, near the banana grove, to make the prison guards think that he had escaped. And so, a search party was formed, to look for the supposed "fugitive" on the beaches of Ubatuba and Caraguatatuba. I had been chosen as I knew all the prisoners and was used to dealing with them. My name is Antonio Francisco Alves. I was known on the island as "Escoteiro". Colonel Paulo Vianna spoke about me in his book. Now, 47 years after the rebellion, I would love to go back, and that's why I've come to ask if you will take me with you" And, taking a deep breath, he said "You have to take me with you!".

It wouldn't have occurred to me to have refused…..here was a truly historical figure, alive, excited, anxious, and the only thing he wanted was to return to where he had lived for so many years.

A few days later we went to Ilha Anchieta.

A cold, fine drizzle accompanied us the whole time. The sea looked like a sheet of grey plastic as the seven schooners, a whole fleet really, made the nine kilometre-crossing to the island.

The normally treacherous "Boqueirao" was also calm. It was very different from that other 20th June, in 1952, when the brave Private Simao Rosa da Cunha had to make his way through the strong current, not by boat, but relying solely on his powerful arms – the arms of a person used to swimming in the sea.

When we reached dry land, I saw that more than 500 people had gathered, despite the bad weather, each eager to experience something special.

After I had been circulating amongst the crowd for about two hours, an ex-soldier, long retired, came up to me and asked, "Have you seen how many people there are here? Did you know that one of them is an ex-prisoner?".

I asked him who it was and he replied, "Escoteiro".

I was surprised when I learned he had been a prisoner at one time but happier than ever.

Yes, "Escoteiro" had been a prisoner on the island, sent there to pay his debt to society for what he had done……..or rather, not done, for, according to him, he had only been the look-out in a gambling den, whose job it was to let the owners know when the police were arriving. He and the others were caught three times by the police officers who came to the casino disguised as postmen, electricians, etc. For this, he was sent to the island, without having stood trial, been sentenced or even charged… nothing.

On account of his good behaviour, his discipline and his usefulness to the prison administration, he came to be employed by the prison authorities and to be completely rehabilitated….when I found out about his prisoner roots, I was even more impressed with what he had done and become.

Many highly dangerous prisoners were sent to the island, but alongside them were many first-offenders, or men considered to be vagrants but who had committed no crime; there were both adults and minors, some had stood trial but others hadn't. They were, of course, all poor men…..the only rich ones were political prisoners who had opposed the government.

"Escoteiro" carried out his duties proudly. He later retired from the (Casa de Custódia e Tratamento de Taubaté). He was fine example of rehabilitation and of what the prison service used to be capable of, and of how a prisoner can be reintegrated into society. Of course, this can only work if the prisoner himself desires it.........

Nota do autor: ("Escoteiro" is the main protagonist of my book "O Prisioneiro do Pavilhao 6 da Ilha Anchieta").

Faria Junior's story
by the author

It can be seen from the prison archives that in 1944 Faria Junior was considered to be a model prisoner, well-behaved, who was never guilty of the slightest breaking of the rules in any of the prisons he was held in. It is said, however, that the reason he was transferred to Ilha Anchieta from the State Penitentiary in 1940 was because he couldn't adapt to discipline. His sentence, at that time, added up to 104 years of prison. He had killed four people. Nobody, including himself, thought he would ever be released.

He was a very strong man, but his right eye was made of glass; he had lost the one he had been born with in a fight with other criminals. As he was considered to be a highly dangerous man, he was never allowed out of the prison itself, not even to do daily chores, like chop wood, and so he worked in the prison laundry, where he stayed several years.

He always made a good impression on those who observed him. He was always clean, recently shaved, short haired and wore clothes that were glistening white, carefully ironed and even starched. He obeyed orders to the letter. But at night he was always locked away in solitary confinement. This was not because he deserved to be punished in this way, but because he himself had asked to be put in solitary because he feared that one of the other prisoners would kill him while he slept. Infamous criminals have to be more careful than the others, because he who has killed another well known criminal has to live with this infamy. And if he himself is killed, no-one is going to ask too many questions..........

With his good behaviour and native intelligence, he petitioned for his sentences to run concurrently. He won his appeal and his sentence was shortened to fifty-odd years, more than twenty of which he had already served.

When the rebellion took place, more than a hundred of the most dangerous criminals escaped on the boat "Carneiro da fonte", leaving behind more than three hundred who couldn't fit on. The barracks had been taken over by the prisoners. Eight military policemen, two civilian workers and several prisoners had been killed. But even more people were destined to die. When the rebels left the island more would die, for the boat on which they escaped was only built to carry sixty, not the hundred-odd who clambered aboard. When the boat began to sink, the heaviest prisoners were thrown overboard to make the boat lighter and were probably eaten by sharks. Despite all this, some rebels did manage to reach the mainland........well, that's another story....you can read about it in the chapter "Rebellion".

Back on the island, there were a group of prisoners who had decided to remain loyal to the authorities and Faria rapidly took on the role of leader. He told his "troops" to round up all the captured policemen, civilian workers and their families and to take them to a cow-shed where they could be protected from the orgy of violence being unleashed by those who hadn't been able to fit onto the boat in which the others had escaped.

Faria Junior armed himself with a rifle and protected the lives of many women and children who were otherwise defenceless.

Later, when this had been documented by the new prison authorities, Faria was rewarded and set free. He left the island in triumph and would only return as a government employee, as a prison guard, a job he held for several years.

He died in Ubatuba, in the Old Age People's Home Sao Vicente de Paula, as a resident and a good man who had dedicated himself to the smooth running of what proved his last home. His burial was attended by the many friends he had made in his final years.

Nota do autor: These facts are collected in the book "The Ilha Anchieta and me" by Colonel Paulo Vianna.

Senhora Nazaré
by the author

On the 29th July 1999, Sergeant Ivan, came to the (to the association of the Officials of the Reservation in the city of Taubaté) where I work as the director of public relations, and invited me to meet some other "Filhos da Ilha".

I agreed at once, and so we went in his battered "fusca" (VW Beetle) to 39, Rua Euclides da Cunha in the neighbourhood Parque Sabará, Tabaté, where we met with Maria Nazaré Vieira, fifty, who, together with her brother Domingos and daughter Áquina, made us very welcome.

As Dona Nazaré spoke with emotion about her father João Damasceno and her mother Benedita Alvina, we told them that we had heard a lot about her parents in the meetings we had had with the survivors of the 1952 mutiny.

We told Dona Nazaré that the "Filhos da Ilha" spoke about (Mr Damasceno and his wife Alvina) , lively musicians and singers would used to entertain the other families on the island with their songs, both at parties and on the "Praínha" where the couple liked to sing while they sat on a big rock beside the sea. During those excursions in the fifties, the adults would listen to the music of Damasceno and his wife while the children swam in the sea.

Dona Nazaré told us that, although she had been born and baptised on the island, what she knows of those days she has learnt from her aunt, Lourdes, as she herself was only three years and five months old at the time of the rebellion. But stories about life on the island were always being reminisced about with great emotion by the family. This had made her want to see those landscapes which populated her mind, where her beloved mother and father had lived so happily with her brothers and aunts and uncles.

Once more I witnessed the mark the island had left on the people who had lived there.

Dona Nazaré told us how hard it had been to adapt to life in Taubaté, where her father, Sergeant Adamasceno, was transferred after the rebellion. The big family had lived amongst the abundance of the island Anchieta, where they had not had to pay rent and there was fish and fruit in abundance. In contrast in Taubaté, they had had to work hard so as not to go hungry, as the city they had suddenly found themselves in only functioned if you had money.

Children who had played happily by the sea, without a care in the world, really felt the difference when they had to go and adapt to life in Taubate and the other towns they were moved to after they left the island.

After 47 years, they are now meeting up with each other again. Many don't recognise each other at first, but, on hearing each other's names, they remember and cry, talking about the times they spent together as children. As we conversed, the time passed very quickly in Dona Nazare's house and, after enjoying some delicious home-made rolls baked by Adamesco's granddaughter, we returned to the Association, happy to have met such a nice family who would henceforth become part of our group, "Filhos da Ilha".

Colonel Helio
by the author

While doing research for this book, many times I met people who had been mentioned in the book written by Colonel Paulo Vianna, the last dirctor of the Ilha Anchieta prison.

On this occasion, we were in the cemetery in, gurilândia, Taubaté, where we had gone to attend the burial of a retired police officer. Looking around at the people who had gathered there to see off their old friend, I caught sight of one of those people mentioned in Colonel Vianna's book. Right there in front of me was Colonel of the Reserve Brazilian Air Force, Helio Ferreira da Silva.

I couldn't resist going over to talk to him; he greeted me warmly and we ended up going for a coffee in the cafeteria in the grounds of the cemetery. I asked him what exactly he had taken with him on those "lightning visits" he had made to the island, and which made those who lived there so happy.

He told me that he had first met Colonel Vianna when they had been teenagers in Taubate and had studied together and that they had been really good friends since then.

When the moment had come for them to choose their professions, Paulo Vianna had chosen the security forces, now called the military police and he, Helio, had chosen the Air Force. By the beginning of the 1950s they had both attained the rank of Captain. While he, as an aviator, could soar the skies like a bird, with so much freedom, PV was confined to the Ilha Anchieta as Prison Director.

To go to the island by land and by sea was an epic undertaking in those days, and so the way in which he could give a gift to his friend from his youth, was to get a number of the day's newspapers and recently published magazines from a newspaper stand in Rio de Janeiro and to make them into a parcel. This parcel would have to be made so well that it wouldn't get damaged either when dropped or if it fell into the sea when he threw it out of the plane as it passed over the island where his friend was working.

He did this many times. He would take off from Rio, make a manoeuvre towards the state of Sao Paulo, and would fly low over the island one, two, three times and the third time drop the package of newspapers and magazines.

Down below the excited children would run after the package, which would sometimes fall into the sea. Captain Helio in his plane would smile as if he were playing a game with the children, who would throw themselves into the water, rescue the parcel and go running with it to Captain Paulo Vianna's house.

Fron left to right: Gabriela, Guilherme, Mara, Gracia e Palma, indo para a Ilha.

PV, would leave his duties to one side and go out onto the veranda where he would wave to thank his friend, who would return immediately to Rio de Janeiro.

PV, when relating this story in his book, entitled the relevant section "They were presents which fell from the sky".

The island today
by the author

Nowadays, people who want to travel the nine kilometres which separate the island from the mainland no longer have to go by canoe as they did in 1952.

Powerful "schooners" belonging to the Mykonos and Corsario companies, who each own several boats, safely transport tourists to and from the island.

Experienced seamen captain the ships. During the crossings the crew often improvise musical entertainment with guitars and percussion to further delight the passengers already marvelling at the wonderful scenery around them. The journey to the island takes about forty minutes.

The further the boat gets away from the mainland, the bluer the sea, and then you can see Ilha Anchieta, completely covered in vegetation, a beautiful green, surrounded by rocks on which the waves break. The rocks give way in places to the most beautiful beaches, seven in all; it is difficult to say which is the loveliest..........

But when you disembark, and look back toward the mainland, it is as if you had never left, for it is difficult to miss the Serra do Mar, rising high above everything else, from the top of which the whole of this part of the coast and its islands can be seen. On the island you find a warm welcome, a snack bar, toilets, a museum and guides who can tell you about the history of the island, the various legends and help you find your way around. The director of the island, Manuel de Azevedo Fontes, and his wife, the biologist Doutora Maria de Jesus, are always available and organise everything so that the visits go smoothly. The sea is usually so clear that you can see shoals of fish swimming around....in fact it is a shame to be there for such a short time – it would be wonderful to be to stay there and live……...

The Tamar Project, which seeks to protect turtles, used to have a place on the island where they showed the tourists the work being done by the project, but today those tanks are empty. The turtles have been taken to the Tamar centre in Itagua, in Ubatuba.

The ruins of the prison are really impressive. Some cells still have their roofs, others don't. The tiles were removed by the local monkeys in order to get at and eat the little spiders. The problem is, they didn't put the tiles back when they had finished (!) and so the rain has rotted the beams and that's why the roofs are collapsing. It didn't help that for many years there was no-one on the island looking after the buildings and so they deteriorated quickly.

When they did do repairs, it was only to the buildings by the sea. There are many other buildings missing roofs but with the walls (remarkably free of cracks) still standing, where you can see things written and drawn by the prisoners who lived there, suffering the bitterness of incarceration, more than 47 years ago. Some of the cells seem to be full of so much negative energy that they drive the most sensitive of us away.

On the floor of one of the cells used for solitary confinement, you can see a phrase left by Gauchao, prisoner number 436; he wrote "You have to have suffered in order to appreciate happiness". The administrative buildings, which lie between the prison ruins and the beach, were recently rebuilt with funds from the World Bank, channelled through Commander Henrique of the Navy, who has a special regard for the island.

The old school building is still there, next to a fig tree which is now more than 50 years old.

The houses which used to belong to the director of the prison, the military commander and a few others, are still in use. The prison director's is now a place where people who come to work on the island can stay.

The little chapel of Senhor Bom Jesus was restored and reopened on 6th August 1999 and will hopefully be used by the faithful for many years to come. Behind the prison, where once the houses of the civilian workers stood, there is just grass. Just a few pillars of the doctor's house remain, half hidden amongst the bushes. Even the bricks have disappeared; maybe they were taken away to be used on the mainland...Many things have changed in these 51 years since the prison was closed...

Only two houses remain from what was the soldiers' part of town, the Vila Militar. They are crumbling, but in one of them you can still see a bit of cloth hanging from the ceiling of one of the rooms. The barracks stood up to the attack of the prisoners and also the ravages of time. The walls have no cracks, even if they are surrounded by vegetation. The roof is nearly intact, but because some tiles are missing the beams have been damaged and are not safe. The watch tower in front of the barracks is surrounded by the thick branches of trees which have been growing all these years and now obscure the once-panoramic view which must have taken in the prison, the director's house, the detachment and the back of the Praia Grande beach.

We believe that now more interest is being shown in the island, there is a good chance that the remaining buildings – of such historical importance - will be saved and can be restored.

Legends...

Sergeant Xavier
by the author

The little girl, Adne, was sitting with her grandfather on the veranda of his house in the centre of Ubatuba when we came to interview him. It was drizzling and was quite chilly. When I introduced myself, Sergeant Reformado Xavier led us into the house.

He was relaxed with us because he had already heard about our project from his son. The other grandchildren gathered around to hear their grandfather tell his stories once again and sat down at our side.

His son, Valdinei, who had taken over the job of looking after the island when his father retired and had now been in this job for 18 years, came and sat down with us. As we were in a hurry we got straight to the point; we asked him to tell us about the island's ghosts.

He smiled and, thinking back, remembered when he was the only person living on the island after the prison was closed, and how he would amuse himself by teasing the tourists who would sometimes spend the night there. After telling them several ghost stories he would wait until it was dark and they were all asleep....all except "Soldado Malvado – the Evil Soldier".

He would tie cans onto a piece of fishing line, and then pull it down off the roof onto the ground, where it would clatter and sound like ghosts walking about....

The poor tourists, silently terrified in their rooms, couldn't wait for the morning to come......The following day some of them would mention to Xavier what they had heard and he would confirm that he too had heard ghost noises during the night....

I felt really disappointed when I heard this because I had been hoping to hear real ghost stories, of UFOs, of all these famous phantoms supposed to inhabit this part of the coast...no-one better than this man, I thought, who had lived on Anchieta for 25 years, for 18 of which he had been completely alone.

Before we left, I decided to try one more time....

This time I was more specific in my request. I asked if he could tell us if he had never seen anything at all that could justify the island's claim to be haunted.. Xavier then assumed a knowing look and gave a little smile, as if he understood what it was I wanted, he made himself comfortable in the armchair and replied, " well, there were three cases....

I was told the first by some fishermen I knew. People whose word could be trusted. They were on one of the island beaches, pulling in their nets, when they saw three or four men get down off a big rock, some five metres high. They descended, talking. They walked along the beach for a bit and then climbed up another rock, another tall one and then.....disappeared into the undergrowth, having taken no notice of the fishermen. But a problem remained...

How had those strangers climbed down and then up those steep, smooth rocks if they were practically upright, vertical? They had done it so naturally, not using their hands to help them, just their feet....".

Another time, Xavier said, he was on walking on the beach at night, when he saw a light, like that of a torch, coming towards him slowly and silently. Xavier stopped still. The light got bigger the nearer it came. He stood stock-still as the light passed by about three metres from him. It was about a metre in diameter. There was no-one holding it, it was just the light by itself…it passed by and disappeared. Xavier couldn't move, he was so terrified, and then, when he'd recovered he went and locked himself in his lodging to think about what had happened, but he has never been able to think of an explanation for what he saw that night.

The third time was when he was hunting one night; it was about 10pm and he was in the middle of the forest when he heard the sound of an axe chopping down a tree. The chopping noise came from about 100 metres away. He then heard the noise of a big tree falling to the ground. Xavier stayed quiet in the hiding place, waiting for the paca (a kind of large South American rodent) that he was hunting. He didn't want to come out of the hide and lose the prey he decided to continue hunting and go and see what had happened with the tree the following day. The next day he returned to see the tree which had been chopped down and …surprise! There was no tree chopped down, nor fallen, and not even any sign that the vegetation had been disturbed.

After hearing these stories, we said goodbye to Xavier and his family and left. I had been really rewarded for my time; I had found out that Anchieta really was a place full of mysteries and stories….

I had already heard the inhabitants of the island talk about the "spirit of the old lady",as they call it…the ghost of one of the owners of land on the island in times gone by, who had to abandon her land by order of the government, probably, it is believed, when they decided to build a prison there in 1908. Later, according to the legend, the lady died and her spirit returned to the land she had loved so much. Nowadays she plays around with the people who live there; untying the mooring ropes of their boats, which float about on top of the waves; she hides keys and other small things which only come to light again when the owner offers up a prayer….For me all these ways of being religious have equal value.

As for the experience with the circle of light, which Xavier saw (a probe, perhaps?), on one of the occasions when he had to leave the island for a while he was replaced by another character in our story, one Private Laudelino Mesquita. He told us that one night, alone on the island, he saw a light on Praia Grande. He thought it must be fishermen and decided to go down to relieve the solitude a bit by having a chat with them. He left the administration building and went down to the beach...

  As he got nearer the beach he noticed that the light was ascending. He began to feel something strange was happening. He got closer and saw that the light was now as high as the trees which surrounded the beach. To make things worse, that light was now coming right up to him, Laudelino. Stock-still, he felt his hair standing on end and his body trembling with fear. He turned on his heels and ran off without looking back. He went into the administration building, locked the door and tried to sleep...he didn't know what it had all meant...today he is a retired sergeant of the Military Police and lives in Ubatuba.

Retired Sergeant Xavier, his granddauters and son, Xavier, in their house in Ubatuba.
(1999)

Island Ghosts

In the past, Messias, who worked on the island, used to use the administration building which is nowadays Dr Maria's room. Somebody told me that he used to keep a ladder in his room, which I found intriguing. When I asked him why, he replied that it was because of the problems that he used to have with his room which occurred every single night.

As soon as he locked the door to his room, it was impossible to open again until daybreak, when, once again, the key would turn in the lock and open the door. When he tried to unlock the door at night, the key would turn round and round in the lock in vain and he could never open the door. That was why he kept a ladder in his room. He would leave the room through the window, using the ladder, in order to do his nightly rounds. When he returned he would climb the ladder to the window to get in. He had to do this every time he did his rounds. Messias doesn't stay there any more. He stays in the hostel with his colleagues. It is very common to hear someone calling one's name, even during the day; this frightens people at first, but you get used to it.

One night, at about 10pm, as I was going to the employees' hostel, called the "Rancho da Amizade", in front of the old prison, I was chatting to a boy walking alongside me, when Aline, one of the young monitors who had been on the island for quite a while, ran up behind us and looked frightened. She said she had heard someone calling her name, had looked over to where the noise had come from but there had been no-one there. I reminded her that this often happened, even in daylight....I am always hearing stories of how people see, for just a brief instant, flashes of people walking or talking, images which suddenly vanish. Some of these people are seen wearing prisoner uniforms.

When I walk past the ruins of the prison at night, I often hear a hum of conversation, like that of prisoners talking. I know what the sound is like as I have worked in several prisons. There is a certain rhythm and tone to the conversations, which is unmistakeable. I always try to make out what the voices are saying, but because of the distance and the fact that several voices are talking at once, it isn't possible.

Some of the monitors say that they are often passing by a door, when it suddenly slams shut, even though there isn't a breeze….

I have heard tales of people being seen in the Vila Militar coming out from the forest and going into the ruins of the houses, but when people go after them to see where they've got to, they have disappeared. I have heard stories of how voices are heard talking inside these same houses, despite the fact no-one can be seen.

There are three places on the island which are particularly full of bad energy; they are, the solitary confinement cells, the isolation unit in the old prison, and the old military detachment on the Morro de Papagaio.

I have told people who are especially sensitive to these things, not to go to these places as they could get dizzy, feel nauseous or get headaches. Dr Ernesto, one of the researchers, took several photos and when he developed them, several shapes could be seen, including skulls, which hadn't been present when he took the photos.

When we began the work of the commission to recover the history of Anchieta in 1998, my wife and I would often feel waves of this energy. Even when just walking from one beach to the other, from the Praia de Presidio to the Praia das Palmas. Now, after several ecumenical and open-air masses, which are celebrated each year when the "Filhos da ilha" get together, we don't feel the same bad energy. At least, only in the three places I mentioned above. The island is a place to be admired, but also respected!

I was sitting a my little table one day where I sign books, when an elderly gentleman came up to me, and said, "You don't know what you are getting yourself into here!".

I understood immediately what he was talking about and replied that I most certainly did….that, apart from the material work we were doing, there was the other question of spiritual healing……I asked him if he knew why an island as beautiful as Anchieta had been destined to be the prison for so many men who had come from so far away, many of whom would die there too…. he replied, "crimes committed at sea will be punished at sea".

That gentleman turned out to be the president of the spiritualist movement "Kardecista", from Silveiras in the eastern part of the Vale de Paraiba.

Antonio from Poruba
by the author

My friend Lieutenant Lamosa, when he found out that I was writing a book about what had happened on the island in 1952, asked me to go and talk to "Seu Antonio do Poruba", an old boatman, who had ferried people around in his boat for many years. He was known as the "Boatman of Poruba", the place near Ubatumirim where the fugitives had seen their boat smashed up, due to the inexperience of Timonchenco, who had taken the helm that day. The boat, "Carneiro da Fonte", had been destroyed by the waves as it arrived at the mainland.

At Poruba, beside the football pitch, which is fenced off with barbed wire, there is a small bar. When I got there I left the car nearby and walked to the bar. Behind the counter there was a man who looked to be about 60, but who must have been older, given what he (I thought it must be him) had done all those years ago....

I asked one of the men who was drinking beer who "Seu Antonio" was and he pointed out the man I had thought it was. I had wanted to arrive discreetly as if in somebody else's house, - I wanted to ask some questions and wasn't sure of what reception I would get.

I introduced myself to Seu Antonio and said that Lieutenant Lamosa had sent me. He came to other end of the bar, where I was standing, in order to hear what I had to say. I asked him what it had been like when the escaped prisoners had arrived there in 1952.

He replied that there had been 84 prisoners, each of them armed. They came and began to talk to him. He was only 20 at that time. The conversation went well. They told him they wanted to get to Rio by following the telephone lines. He was showing them the way and giving them instructions when a friend of his passed by and saw all those strangers, armed as they were. Thinking they were police officers and, wanting to be friendly he asked, "O Antonio, have you met up with your colleagues?"

One of the prisoners was confused and asked, "Colleagues? Why did he say "colleagues?"

Antonio's friend said, "Aren't you policemen? Antonio works for the state too!"

The prisoners said nothing and Antonio's friend, sensing he had put his foot in it, left....Antonio worked for the local council and took people over in his boat..........but the fugitives didn't like the idea of anyone working for the government, even if not exactly a policeman himself, it was all the same to them. The upshot was that Antonio had to carry 84 prisoners across the river on his back as a punishment......

Not content with this punishment, the fugitives decided to give poor Antonio a good thrashing and thrash him they did. One of them, seeing that Antonio had fallen on his back onto the ground, knelt down and, with one knee each side of Antonio, began to strangle with him with both hands. At that moment there appeared, no-one knows where he came from, an old man, still strong, pale-skinned, with grey hair. He was wearing white trousers and a white shirt and carried a piece of branch as a stick, with which he began to beat the prisoner who was strangling Antonio, until he let go. The other prisoners looked on without wanting to get involved and said nothing.

The man dressed in white, after reprimanding the prisoners, took Antonio down a path through the forest and got away without the prisoners following them. Once they were a safe distance away, the man in white took Antonio by the shoulders and stood in front of him saying.

"Go, son! And don't look behind you. Without understanding what was going on, he walked a few paces away from the old man, but, overcome with curiosity, risked having a peek. He turned round and looked. The forest was completely quiet and the there was no sign on the path of the man in white......

Antonio asked around in his neighbourhood. He wanted to know who it was who had saved him from certain death. Nobody knew. Nobody had seen or even heard of that man in white. A few days later Antonio went to give thanks at the cathedral of Aparecida de Norte. He went to thank the saint, of whom he was a devoted follower. When "Seu Antonio" finished telling me this story, his eyes were wet with tears.... I thanked him and left the bar in the direction of my car......

Senhora Adélia
by the author

One day when I arrived at the AORPM, Vinicius, the secretary, gave me a fax which had come about Ilha Anchieta. I wanted to read it straight away and so I went to my room to read it. I unrolled the fax and read:

By Adelia for Lieutenant Samuel

I, Adelia de Araujo, daughter of Amaro Lourenco de Araujo and Maria Aparecida de Araujo, began my life in the following way, according to my mother.

When she was nine months pregnant, mother found herself at the top of the Morro de Papagaio one night, in the dark, as there wasn't electricity on that side of the island. She was beginning to have contractions and had gone there to shout for my father to come. She came across a couple who were walking towards her with a torch. The couple quickly escorted her to her home and went to get my father. When my father got there he put her face down, maybe because he was nervous or maybe it was just that he had no experience of these things, and went off to get the midwife, Dona Ana, Seu Pinda's wife.

By the time he returned with her, I had been born, but the placenta was still intact. Dona Ana saw to my mother and cleaned up after the birth. During the next few days, Dona Ana's daughters, Maria and Gracia, were a great help to my mother. They took it in turns to wait on her and get whatever she needed.

Gracia married Captain Palma, who has now passed away.

When I was about two months' old I was christened in the Little chapel on the island, the "Capelinha", and my godparents were Cornelia and Artur Militao. When I was two we moved to the Vila Militar. At that time there was an abundance of coconuts on the island, which were usually picked and collected up by the prisoners. As far as provisions went, it was difficult to buy them. My parents went to the Enseada beach in Ubatuba, or even as far as Taubate to get them.

The prisoners were always nice to us. They liked to play around with me, calling me by my nickname, "Preta" They went fishing with the soldiers and with my father too.

When I returned to Anchieta after 45 years away, I was overcome with emotion. I couldn't stop crying, both from happiness and sadness. A pain stabbed through my chest and I thought I was about to die. Anchieta continues to be beautiful and wonderful, despite what happened there on 20th June 1952. Anchieta calms the spirit, it is direct contact with nature – sea, sky and forest. On returning there with the "Filhos da Ilha", I realised how much I loved the place where I had been born.

Adelia de Araújo

IV - First Observation
by Senhora Gracia

On the 20th June 1998, on the anniversary of the mutiny, I took part in an excursion to Ilha Anchieta, in order to lay flowers on the memorial, in homage of all those who laid down their life in the line of duty. We were met by Dr Manoel de Azevedo Fontes e Dr^a Maria de Jesus Robin, who was in charge of use of public lands. We were thus made aware of the new environmental policy and the importance put on preservation nowadays.

After we had visited all the buildings, we were taken to the patio of the prison where we were given a detailed explanation of all the aims of the programmes adopted for the island. The discussion was thrown open and we were asked if anyone had anything to say. Since no-one had, I said that I wished to make a comment to Dr Manoel said that I couldn't resign myself to the fact that the church which had been so important to us in the past, and of which I had such happy memories, had been converted into a souvenir shop. I begged, in the name of all the Catholics present, that the church should be returned to its previous glory. Dr Manoel listened carefully and promised to send my complaint to his superiors. I began to think of all the problems I had caused with my request, but faith, as they say, moves mountains and so I thought that the Good Lord might hear my request.

At no time did I think that my desire to rescue the church could have any connection with the Holy bible, the part which deals with the merchants in the Temple, and how Jesus expelled the Pharisees and the place reverted to being a place of prayer. From then onwards there were lots of difficulties but in the end the chapel was turned back into a church. On the 20th June 1999, after 47 years, a mass was once again celebrated in the chapel, this time by Frei Gastone Pozzobom.

Later on, when the chapel had been beautifully restored, now with an image of Jesus and Santo Expedito, the patron saint of the Military Police, with a new altar and screen, a Mass was celebrated on 6th August 1999 on the day of the Transfiguration of Christ by the Bishop Frei Dom Fernando Mason.

I was extremely happy and satisfied to witness my contribution to the church and to the island.

A view of the pier and administration building on the Island. (1999)

Praia do Presídio and, behind it, Praia Grande. (1999)

Meeting of the chapel rescue committee, with Ubatuba Mayor, Zizinho. (1999)

From left to right: Lenina, Ten. Lamosa, Dr^a. Mara, Dra. Maria de Jesus, Gracia, Zizinho, Cap. Palma, Dr. Anoel e Frei Gastone. (1999)

"Escoteiro" showing the "isolation" where "Portuga" was locked up at night. (1999)

"Escoteiro" with the journalist PedroMantoan, film-maker Araken and technician Odair, of Rede Globo. (1999)

The island on TV
by the author

Towards the end of July 1999, I received a phone call from the regional editor of the Globo television channel, Levy Soares de Lima. He was interested in producing some material to be broadcast on the morning of 8th August. The coverage would extend to the whole of the state of Sao Paulo on the programme "Antena Paulista".

We couldn't miss this opportunity and so I rushed around contacting Senhor Antonio Francisco Alves, better known as "Escoteiro", and Captain Palma and his wife Gracia. I also organised our crossing to the island on board one of the schooners belonging to the company "Mykonos", which has always helped us out.

And so, on the 4th August, we were all gathered together along with the TV Globo crew; the reporter Paedro Montoan, the cameraman Arakem and the technician Odair.

"Escoteiro" was beside himself with excitement; finally he was getting to tell the story which he knew so well, the story of his life, really, to thousands of people in the whole state watching on television. Senhora Gracia, who had lived on the island with her family when she was a child, tried to keep her emotions in check so as to not to cry in front of the cameras.

When we arrived at the Saco da Ribeira, we boarded the schooner Maria Konga and set sail for Ilha Anchieta.

There were several other people on board, amongst them an old friend of mine, Lieutenant Lamosa, who is dedicated to the island project and who was travelling to Anchieta too, though for different reasons. He was taking to the little chapel, senhor Bom Jesus, its first bell, which had been donated by the owner of Marina Golden Port, senhora Erothides.

Once on the island we worked hard under a blistering hot sun, but we were all excited about what we were doing and the fact that finally our efforts would be crowned with success. Finally, after 47 years, what had happened on the island would be revealed, related by those who had actually been there lived through the rebellion.

We visited everything, including the solitary punishment cells where the prisoner number 436, "Gauchao", had carved out the phrase, using some sharp instrument, "It is necessary to know suffering in order to appreciate happiness".

They also filmed the isolation cells, in one of which the prisoner Alvaro Carvalho Farto, better known as "Portuga", had stayed every night for months, at his own request, alleging that he was frightened the other prisoners wanted to kill him. In this way he had the peace and quiet necessary to plan all the details of the rebellion. (See the chapter, "Rebellion").

On the day of the filming, at around 3pm, when we were absolutely starving, Maria Jose, on of the employees, came and invited us to have lunch.

Obviously, we accepted the invitation at once.

When we got to the table, she kept apologising for the simplicity of the meal: rice, beans and fried fish. We said nothing. We couldn't – we were too busy eating to speak. What a delicious meal that was!

At 4pm we said goodbye on the pier and thanked her for her hospitality. We had finished filming and now had to wait until the morning of 8th August to see the fruits of our labour. On the way back, we ran into Lieutenant Lamosa again, who had spent his time on the island that day hanging the bell on a chain from one of the beams in the chapel.

The programme was broadcast and was even commented on by the journalist, Joelmir Beting and the writer from Ubatuba, Washington de Oliveira, the "Filinho da Farmacia", who said, "From time to time, Ilha Anchieta, which used to be known as Ilha dos Porcos, gets back in the papers again!".

Cap. Palma and Dona Gracia, windswept on the boat Tapira. (1999)

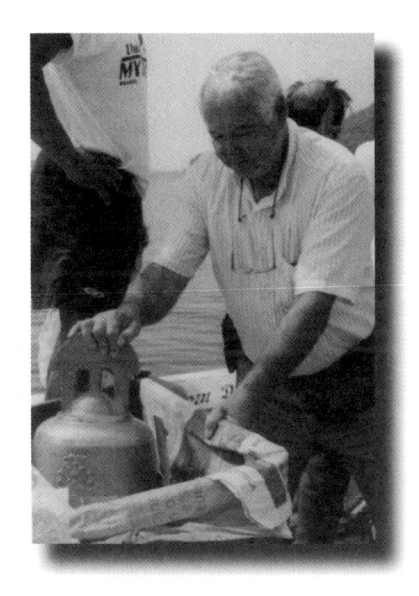

Ten. Lamosa taking the bell to the Chapel. (1999)

Cap. Palma and the owner of the Mikonos Company, Alexandre Jean Antonakis. (1999)

The schooner Vera Cruz returning to the mainsland after taking the bell to the chapel on the Island. (1999)

Municipal guards from Ubatuba carrying the new statue of Jesus to the chapel. (1999)

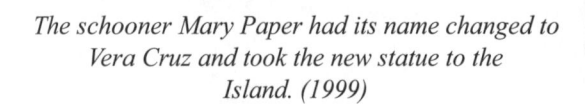

The schooner Mary Paper had its name changed to Vera Cruz and took the new statue to the Island. (1999)

Erothides de Oliveira Godoy. (1999)

Erothides de Oliveira Godoy and her son Godoy, owners of Marina Golden Port, in Saco da Ribeira. (1999)

The re-opening of the chapel
by the author

On the 6th August 1999 the sun shone brightly.

At 7am we gathered in front of the (association of the Officials of the Reservation in the city of Taubaté). We had organised an excursion to Anchieta for that important day. I and my wife Mara, lieutenant Lázaro and his wife Maria Helena, secretary Vinicius boarded the bus and left. This time there was just the one bus from Taubate, we hadn't asked for a police escort and we went via Caraguatatuba.

Lieutenant Bernardino, his wife Zelia, Captain Clovis, Lieutenant Vale and Lieutenant Faria ahd all gone down the day before. They were going to prepare the lamb barbeque we were all looking forward to. Captain Palma and his wife, Gracia, had also gone on ahead, in order to welcome, presidente of A.O.R.R.P.M. Colonel Edilberto de Oliveira Melo, and family who were coming from Sao Paulo. We arrived at Saco de Ribeira and got on the boat around 11am.

We made the crossing in the schooner "Maria Conga" belonging to the Mykonos shipping company. When we got to the island we saw that the celebration of the mass, by (Bispo Don Fernando Mason) was well underway. It was taking place in the patio of the old prison as not everybody would have been able to fit into the little chapel. Also present were (Frei Gastone Possobom, Prefeito de Ubatuba Zizinho Vigneron, Senhora Erothides de Oliveira Godoy, Dr José Luiz de Carvalho, Dr Manoel de Azevedo Fontes and Dr[a] Maria de Jesus Robin).

After the Mass, a very lively Happy Birthday" was sung for Dr[a] Maria de Jesus, whose birthday it was, the same day as that of our patron saint. In his speech the mayor gave us a real history lesson about Brazil (well, he is a historian!), focussing especially on Ubatuba and the Ilha Anchieta. The chapel was now being used again, but would have to wait for the new millennium to be remodelled according to the plans drawn by the famous architect of the early twentieth century, Ramos de Azevedo, found in the archives. At least, that is what some people would like. Others want it to stay as it has always been. I believe that when the prison was made, the chapel was left as it was, no-one dared alter it, not even to give it the structure desired by Ramos de Azevedo.

Today, the way things are going, just about everybody thinks the chapel should be left as it is.

We visited the chapel which was looking very beautiful; it had been painted in a delicate peach, with new pews, and on the alter there was an statue of Senhor Bom Jesus on one side and, on the other side, an image of Santo Expedito, the patron saint of the military police, carved in wood by the local artist "Da Mota".

So, the dream of the "Filhos da Ilha" had been realized, to see the chapel restored where many had been baptized, where others had got married, and many of those who were there remembered when Padre Hans Beli, known as Padre Joao, used to come from Ubatuba to celebrate Mass and hear the confessions of the ones who were Catholic. Padre Joao always brought a film with him to show the children after the mass. He would get really angry when the "little ones" got impatient and began to ask to see the film before the mass had finished.

Now, 47 years later, those children are, on average, 50 or 60 years old. They feel happy to have their chapel back in use and they thank those who have given importance to what they lived through, and who have fought to preserve the names of those who paid so dearly.

Journalists Estela and Hélio Rodrigues of TV Globo covered this event too for the programme "Vanguarda Paulista". Many thanks from all of us!

Island Anchieta - Rebellion, the Truth and the Legends 121

Mass celebrating the restoration of the chapel in 06 de agosto de 1999.

Journalist Gilson, from Band Vale, interviewing Lieutenant Lamosa, head of the Ubatuba Council. Stading between them, Milton Vieira, president of the corporals and privates. (1999)

Front row: journalist Gilson and Santinho. Back row: Sargento Faria, Milton Vieira and councillor of Lorena, Vaguinho. (1999)

Next to the mast, in the cap, the senhor Moisés, friend of PM from São José dos Campos, taking part in the celebration.

From left to right: Cabo Santinho, Sgt. Ruiz, Sgt. Faria, President Milton Vieira, Ten. Samuel, councillor Vaguinho. Seated: Cel. Oliveira Jr, diretor de Relações Públicas dos Oficiais da Reserva de Jacareí. (1999)

From left to right: Sgt. Fragoso (Biguá), Ten. Luz, Cel. Edilberto, Cap. Palma, Ten. Turibio and Ten. Mário (Cobrinha). (1999)

The restored chapel, seen from the front. (1999)

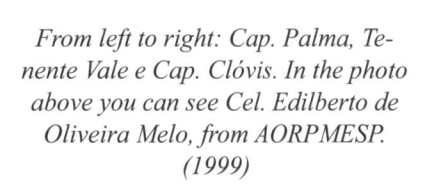

From left to right: Cap. Palma, Tenente Vale e Cap. Clóvis. In the photo above you can see Cel. Edilberto de Oliveira Melo, from AORPMESP. (1999)

From left to right: Sailor João, assistant Mara and tourist from Araguari (MG), inside one of the mikonos schooners moored on the beach Sete Fontes. (1999)

Barbeque

After the presentation of the newly restored chapel, we gathered in the hostel lounge where the military police historian, Colonel Edilberto de Oliveira Melo met someone very important for our project, Dr José Luiz de Carvalho, who is in charge of the 12 state parks in São Paulo, including Anchieta.

Colonel Rodrigues Silva Lopes commander of 20º BPMI was also present.

Reserve Lieutenant Jose Bernadino dos Santos was in charge of lunch; he is a man who possesses two great gifts.

1) he knows all there is to know about how to obtain legal concessions from the military police. Most of us have no idea and so we go to him when we need advice.

2) he makes the best barbeques I have ever had. When he does it, the meat is wonderfully tender and a meal prepared by Bernadino is really something special. I hope you, the reader, will get a chance to have one someday.

Epilogue

All the work done with the wit association of class of Police Military an almost impossible objective in mind, was, I think, inspired by God, and led us to get as far as we have.

A huge effort was made by many to find a story which belongs to each and every one of us. Military police, civil servants, housewives, those who were children in 1952, now adults….everyone linked to this event in the past.

It is wonderful to see the enthusiasm when they get together to record what happened on Ilha Anchieta, in the municipality of Ubatuba. It is half paradise, half hell…a place which has left its mark on us all.

We have given the name "Filhos da Ilha" to all those who, in whatever way, have come to represent the group of people who destiny threw together to live again the moments they lived all those years ago.

Caught between beauty and danger, the island keeps alive the images in the memories of those who lived there.

We are coming to the end of this book, where we have tried to describe what really happened in the words of those who survived the rebellion. Other books have been left to us by those who went before, and they deserve all our respect for they have contributed a lot to our research. In this book, previous testimonies have been checked and confirmed, written down by those who actually lived through the good times and the bad times. All these events had remained in their minds and hearts until now.

As a consequence of this book, many things have come to light after 46 years, many interesting tales and powerful emotions, in our quest to know exactly what happened on Ilha Anchieta, to analyse and to understand. The events of 1952 even attracted a the interest of movie directors; the film "Blood on their hands" (Maos Sangrentas) was made starring Tonia Careiro, Costinha and other actors who were famous at that time. The original, or so we have been told, is in Italy; there are copies in Brazil but they are difficult to get hold of.

The film was shot on a different island. They changed the names of the main protagonists, Pereira Lima and Portuga , but it is not clear why. In the film, the prison director appears dressed in the uniform of Security Forces, but he was a captain of the Army reserve and, in real life, didn't wear any uniform. Despite these differences, the film was good for its time and shows us how widespread interest in the rebellion was, inspiring several books and pages of newspaper coverage.

The events continue to evoke interest. We heard from more than seventy survivors, most of whom are now more than sixty years old and who have contributed immensely to this little book of mine. We couldn't have let this chance go by! Ilha Anchieta is a legendary place through which Indians, Portuguese caravels, planes, UFOs, foreigners and Brazilians have all passed.........it leads us to history, legends and myths.

It drifts through time, kissed by the waters blue as the sky of the Atlantic, caressed by that warm, but cooling breeze which blows off the sea. From time to time, it is lashed by a strong, dangerous north-east wind, and the fishing boats take shelter in the bay in the early mornings. It wraps itself around you, the prey, captive. Like a mermaid, who has absorbed its mysteries, dreaming or awake, you will dream of her.

It is not for nothing that the great cacique Cunhambebe, of the Tupinambas, chose to live there. Since that time, everyone has wanted to possess the island, but she will never belong to anyone! She belongs to all of us, as Dr Manoel, the ex-director says. Or do we all, rather, belong to her? As we have said…all pass through, indigenous tribes, foreigners, Brazilians……she is the only one who remains, imperious and beautiful.

From left to right: Dona Zélia, Ten. Bernadino, Ten. Guimarães ande Ten. Lázaro, in Island Anchieta. (1999)

From left to right: Tenentes Lázaro, Luz and Araújo. (1999)

Comissão Pró Resgate Histórico da Ilha Anchieta

Instituída em 18 - 05 - 98 na sala de reunião do Comando do 5° BPM/I, na Cidade de Taubaté.

(Com abreviaturas militares)

Ten Cel PM PAULO CÉSAR MÁXIMO - Comandante do 5° BPM/I
Presidente

Major PM LAMARQUE MONTEIRO- Sub Comandante do 5° BPMI
Vice- Presidente

Cap Res PM WILSON PRADO PALMA
Representando a A.O.R.P. M - Taubaté

Ten Res PM JOSÉ LÁZARO RIBEIRO
Representando a A.O.R.P. M - Taubaté

Ten Res PM SAMUEL MESSIAS DE OLIVEIRA
Relações Públicas da A.O.R.P. M - Taubaté

Ten Res PM BENEDITO MARTINS DE CASTRO
Representando a A.S.S.P. M - Taubaté

Subten Res PM JOSÉ BENEDITO FARIA SODRÉ
Representando a A.S.S.P. M - Taubaté

1° Sgt Fem Ref PM NANCI RIBEIRO DA SILVA CAMPOS
Representando a A.S.S.P. M - Taubaté.

MARA CRISTINA PEREIRA DE OLIVEIRA
Advogada – OAB – Pindamonhangaba / SP

Soldado PM MILTON VIEIRA
Representando a Associação dos Cabos e Soldados

GRACIA APARECIDA PRADO PALMA
Representando os filhos da Ilha Anchieta

MARIA AYDÊE CARDOSO
Representando as esposas da Ilha

Collaborators: Waltinho Cardoso Filho; film-maker and reporter Sd PM Afonso Alves Júnior; secretary Vinicius Proença and hte photographer Fernando Catuçaba.

Yhe morning of the signing of the first edition, on Ilha Anchieta. In the photo, Lieutenant Samuel and his wife Doctor Mara.

Sailor Mário. He brought us back to the mainland in this boat, throug the rough waters of the Boqueirão. (1999)

A wedding

I was delighted to receive an invitation to the wedding of Cintia and Wilson on the 18th December 1999 at 2pm.

I had been excited about this invitation as it would be the first to be celebrated on Ilha Anchieta in 47 years, as, after the prison shut its gates for the final time in 1955, the chapel was used as a store-room and later as souvenir shop.

It took some tough social and political negotiating on the part of the Pos-Resgate Commission to get it re-opened.

That is why we were overjoyed that this wedding was to be held there.

Our congratulations to the bride and bridegroom, Wilson Alves dos Santos and Cintia Aparecida da Silva, now man and wife. Your names will go down in history!

The best man, special guest and bridesmaid were Lieutenant Lamosa, Dr Manoel e Dr^a Maria. The wedding was conducted by Frei Gastone Possobom from the parish of Ubatuba.

The enf of first edition.

130 — Island Anchieta - Rebellion, the Truth and the Legends

From left to right: the bride Cintia, Friar Gastone and the bridegroom Wilson. (1999)

The bride Cintia and Lamosa, the best man. (1999)

Bride and bridegroom Wilson Alves dos Santos and Cintia Aparecida. (1999)

Appendix to the 2nd edition
Dr Modesto Naclerio Homen

One day, when I arrived at Ilha Anchieta, one of the park monitors gave me a note which contained the address of the teacher Zilda Naclerio Homen, who lived in the Cerqueira Cesar neighbourhood in the city of Sao Paulo. In the note she said that she had kept, for the last 49 years, a copy of the appeal to the Military Court against the conviction of Lieutenant Odwaldo and others for being responsible for the lapses in security which led to the 1952 rebellion.

As soon as I arrived home in Pindamonhangaba, I got in touch with the Professora Zilda and she sent me by post a copy of the Appeal number 1.527 written by her father, the lawyer Dr Modesto Naclério Homem.

Dr Modesto mentioned a list of problems at the island prison, such as a shortage of transport, of help, of workers, of doctors, of nurses. He talked about how the prisoners all lived communally, day and night, when they should have been in cells. Instead they spent their time playing football, listening to the radio, playing guitar, swimming, fishing, fighting, plotting and having sex with each other. There was also a shortage of workshops and teachers.

In the words of Dr Naclerio.

"Low windows looking on to the main passageway is what made the detachment vulnerable to attack".

The Lieutenant, Odwaldo Silva, had asked for the windows of the arms and munitions store to be bricked up and for a watchtower to be built to protect the guards, but these requests were never carried out. He asked for the prison radio (PYH2) to be repaired urgently as it was totally useless and was the only way of communicating quickly with the mainland, but this too was ignored.

He insisted that the number of men and weapons should be increased as there were incredibly few for such a high number of prisoners on such a big island of 316 alqueires (about 7.5 square kilometres) and that, without them, it would be impossible to control. The prison had a civilian director and civilian workers, over whom the military commander had no authority. These men went firing their guns all over the island whenever they felt like it, even though one of the main signals of alarm to attract help from the garrison is usually the sound of gunfire.

The lawyer cites more failings and then concludes, "They have managed to find scapegoats onto whom they have put all responsibility for the rebellion, forgetting all the failings in security of the prison and the failure of the authorities to take essential steps in this regard." "These failings were key factors in the success of the mutiny and so it is most unjust to find the men appealing here against their conviction guilty or responsible in any way."

Dr Naclerio added; "In the debates we have had in the chamber, the prisoners' defence lawyers have said exactly the same thing, that, given so many problems with security at the prison, it would have been impossible for these men to have prevented the mutiny, and for this reason they should be absolved of all responsibility".

The Appeal Court judges judged the accusations against the accused to be groundless and immediately released the following men from custody; lieutenant Odwaldo Silva, Corporal Walter Cardoso, Soldiers José Salomão das Chagas, José Maria, Darcy Vargas de Oliveira, Eudardo Sene, Benedido da Silva e Antonio Marcelino Ribeiro.

Here we wish to do justice to Dr Modesto Naclério Homem publishing his photo:

Dr. Modesto Naclério Homem

The padlock
by the author

While doing the rounds of the launch of the first edition of this book, we were in Pindamonhangaba on the 15th August 2001 at the Clube Literario and Recreativo at around 8pm.

It was really nice to see so many people there; friends, survivors of the rebellion, presidents and directors of the association, retired teachers, representatives of the (two Masson shops, Shop Harmonia e Trabalho and shop Emilio Ribas), as well as colleagues from the newspapers, Jornal da Cidade, Tribuna do Norte and the radio station radio Difusora, and my wife and children.

Later in the evening, when the survivors had come up to the microphone and told us their moving stories about their lives on Anchieta, a young lady carrying a baby, got up and came towards us without saying anything. Her name was Carmen Lydia Pamplin Rodrigues. She was holding a package and an envelope and she handed them to me. She stayed by my side while I opened the package and took out an enormous padlock, with a twisted shackle.

I opened the envelope which contained a sheet of paper saying:

"For Lieutenant Samuel

This padlock belonged to the prison at Anchieta. It was broken open at the time of the rebellion.

My uncle was the prison dentist and lived on the island with his wife Gessy Luporini Nessy.

On the day of the mutiny, my aunt happened to be in Sao Paulo and my uncle, who was liked very much everybody, but especially by the prisoners, was spared and even protected by them.

He kept this padlock for many years as a souvenir and then gave it to me. Today, I would like to donate it, with much affection, to record yet one more chapter in this important story.

Sao Jose dos campos 12/8/2001
Regiane Luporini Zaitune"

I don't need to say how much this meant to me and to all those present who had been listening to the survivors' tales. In particular, I don't know how to thank Regiane Luporini Zaitune, the wife of my friend Pamplin's brother-in-law.

The gift of this padlock was a symbol for me; a kind of passport which confirms my destiny.

Lieutenant Samuel

Journalist Pedro Mantoan, of Rede Globo de Televisão, interviewing the author Lieutenant Samuel, in Ilha Anchieta. (1999)

Prison dentist Armando Nery

Schooner Maria Conga, belonging to the company Miknos. (1999)

Here is how the chapel would have been built according to design Ramos de Azevedo.

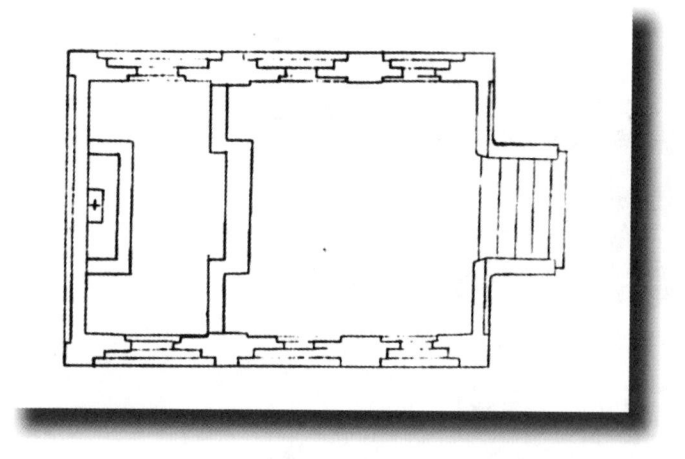

*Above: Ramos's design for the chapel.
Underneath: map showing.*

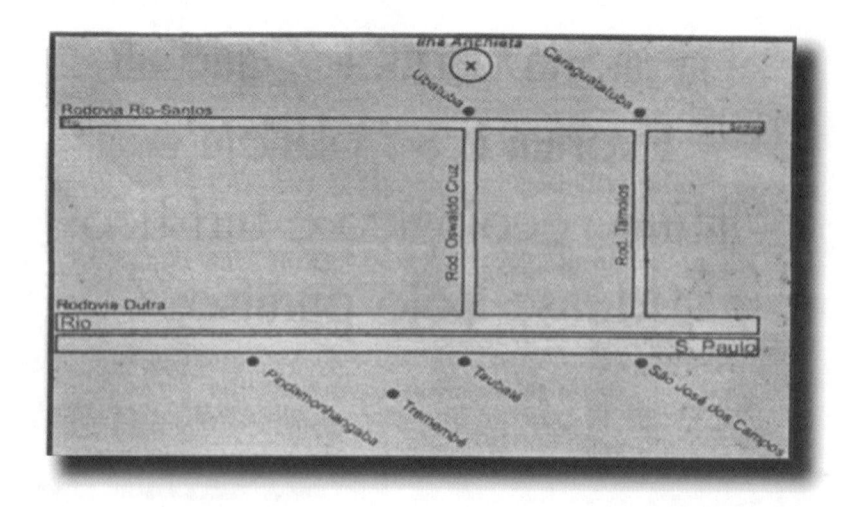

Edgard Malegne Sophia
Um dos capturadores de Pereira Lima e Jirico

One day I went to the capital, Sao Paulo, accompanying my friend Corporal Marcos, who worked with the Fire Service in Pindamonhangaba. He had been promoted and had to change his ID card from Private to that of Corporal.

Early that morning I went to the Association of Sao Rafael in the neighbourhood of Pouso Frio and caught up with the couple Marcos and Eliane, the directors. Together, we all went to Administrative centre of the the Military police, better known as the "Panelao", located in the Avenida Cruzeiro do Sul. When we got there, Marcos had to have his photo taken, so we went to the second lieutenants' and sergeants' association where the photos were taken.

While I was waiting for him, I went to the room where the president of the association was and went to invite him to come with us to the island on 23rd June when we were going with the survivors to pay homage to our heroes who had given their lives.

As I was speaking to the president of the ASSPM, I heard a voice from the next table asking, "Are you talking about the Ilha Anchieta? I was there in 1952".

I asked the gentleman who had spoken why he had gone there and he told me that he had been a member of the platoon, under the command of Lieutenant Nestor, which had gone to capture Joao Pereira Lima. He also said that he had kept photos and newspaper cuttings all these years.

We were really pleased we had met each other and made plans to meet up again.

This next meeting was in the Batallion of Taubate and this time he brought with him the following article from the newspaper "A Hora" dated 09/07/1952:

"CAPTURE OF PEREIRA LIMA A ROUTINE MATTER"

This is the truth about the action which led to the re-capture of the rebel thought to be the leader of the mutiny. It is a surprising account by the soldiers of the 5th battalion. There was no talk of heroics and the soldiers don't want to make too much of what was an ordinary day's work".

This was the main headline in "A Hora" on the 9th July 1952, where, relating the material which had been published in the newspaper "A Tribuna" from Taubate, it says:

The reporter from the newspaper from the Vale de Paraiba overheard conversation in the main square of Taubate between soldiers from the 5th Battalion. One of those overheard was the Corporal Mario de Oliveira Monteiro. His words were confirmed by the detectives and other soldiers present.

"At 2pm on the first of July – said the soldiers – we arrived at Cunha, from where we set out in the direction of Monjolo, where we found a prisoner who had been captured by an army sergeant, of the 5th RI from Lorena. The prisoner was one of the fugitives from Anchieta, known as "Mocoroa", and had been interrogated by Lieutenant Benedito Augusto de oliveira and Dr Nicolau Mario Centola, ther police chief. This prisoner had told them where they would be able to find Joao Pereira Lima and "Jerico", the only ones left of the group which Mocoroa had been separated from when he was re-captured. On Police Chief Centola's instructions, we went to the place he had been told, to the right of the road which links Cunha with Monjolo. At a certain point on the road, Dr Centola sent off into the forest those of us he had chosen to try and capture the two fugitives. That is, myself, six soldiers, and three detectives from the police unit , "Vigilancia e Capturas", Hernani Dantas de Gama, Luis Esteves Barbosa and Arlindo barbosa. We went into the forest, having first left a circle of men in the surrounding bushes to prevent the prisoners from escaping.

Caught at last

After walking into the forest for about twenty minutes, Private Sinfronio Pinheiro da mata caught sight of Joao Pereira Lima and Jerico, squatting under a sheet of iron, hidden by the trees. Straight afterwards, the soldiers Lázaro de Brito Araújo, Benedito Ribeiro da

Silva e Francisco Soares appeared, and backed up their colleague, ordering the fugitives to give themselves up. JPL and J didn't show the least sign of resistance and handed themselves over to the ten men who had come to capture them, who had all gathered in this location.

He didn't fight till the last bullet

Not a shot had been fired. The soldiers found that the two prisoners had a loaded "Winchester" and a "Colt" revolver, as well as lots of ammunition for both weapons. They did not fight till the last bullet, as their fellow-prisoners who had already been captured said they would. There were no heroics, or anything like that. It was one of the simplest arrests, very different form what everybody had expected.

The handover to Dr Centola

Once the prisoners had been caught and disarmed, Dr Nicolau Centola was informed in accordance with the instructions they had been given. Only now did he enter the forest and take charge of the prisoners, taking them to Monjolo with him in an ordinary car with a military escort. When they got there they were handed over to the army, who had instructions from Dr Centola that those of us who had actually caught them, shouldn't be allowed to go near them now. I don't think it was necessary fro him to have said that. At the end of the day, it's not our job to criticise. We had done our duty, and done it well."

Someone commented that it hadn't been fair that the photos of the men who had actually caught the two criminals had not been published in the newspapers. A soldier who, up to then, hadn't said anything, and who we later found out was Edgard Malegne Sophia, replied. "We are not interested in making a splash in the papers or having our photos published. We did what we had been asked to do and all we want is for the name of our Corporation and our Company to be honoured. It was all in the line of duty."

Author's note: this article from "A Hora" which had been lovingly saved all these years, was photocopied and given to me personally by Lieutenant EMS himself, in the inside patio of the 5th BPMI on 20th June 2001, during the annual commemoration which is held for the "Filhos de Ilha".

Our Godfather

I received a phone call from Antonio Braga, son of the ex-Private Geraldo Braga, one of the soldiers who had been part of the prisoner escort on Ilha Anchieta that fatal day, 20th June 1952. Antonio Braga told me that he had written a few lines about the "Filhos da Ilha", and he insisted that I should see them.

I agreed to do so, and I arranged to meet him in the Bairro de Gurilandia in Taubate.

We met and went to his house. His family made me feel most welcome and we began to talk about the thing that interested us most, Ilha Anchieta.

I put on a video of the documentary about the world's largest mutiny, made by the Department of communication in the University of Taubate (Unitau), and we all sat there in the living room with our eyes glued to the screen until it had finished.

After a long conversation over coffee, accompanied by other members of the Braga family, I went home, taking with me the Manuscript by Antonio Braga, where I read the following:

Our Godfather

So much happiness, so many emotions…

I started off crying but then found my tears had been replaced by a big smile, full if peace and happiness.

These are the emotions I feel after returning to the Ilha Anchieta, where I was born, after 49 long years.

This is what we feel, not just me, but many other "Filhos da Ilha" too.

Born again, thanks to the effort, dedication, courage and skill of the person we all affectionately call "Lieutenant Samuel".

All of us "Filhos da Ilha" should not forget the hard work which he has put into this project; many times leaving his chores to one side, moments which he should have spent with his family, in order to sort through all the material about the true story of Ilha Anchieta, looking for survivors and their families who were there and who lived through the horror of that day.

Lieutenant Samuel, after years and years of searching, managed to reunite many of us from that time and to write a book which is so true, neither inventing things nor leaving out any important facts.

Not only did he do this but he also managed to do something else; to bring together so many of us, children of the heroes of that day, to go and visit the island again. This was an excursion which served to increase the bonds between us, reuniting young and old people; it was particularly interesting for us to see the book which he has published.

I am sure that this feeling of mine is shared by every child, every grandchild, every friend, who would all like to thank Lieutenant Samuel for all that he has done.

Our thanks go too to Colonel Paulo Maximo, who has given lots of support to this event, lots of effort, and who has made great sacrifices, giving up his spare time, his time he would have spent relaxing with his family, joining forces with Lieutenant Samuel, so that we can have these marvellous times on Anchieta, every year...There will, I am sure, be other books written by other authors, other tales will be published, but none will be comparable to that of the indefatigable Lieutenant Samuel.

His book highlights the role of each person, from the most humble worker to the highest ranked soldier.

So that no book will be published in the future which says," I was the true hero or the Rambo of Ilha Anchieta".

Our eternal thanks to Samuel and also to his wonderful wife, because I know that she and their children have been robbed of many outings and trips so that other "children" could benefit – the Children of the Island. Today my wife Damaris, my daughter Stella, my sons Diego and Etiene, as well as my granddaughter Isabel, know the history of that paradise called Anchieta.

Thank you, Lieutenant Samuel and family.
Thank you, Colonel Paulo Maximo and family.

Antonio Braga

When I had read this, I felt that all our work to recover the story of the rebellion and the island – which had been in danger of being forgotten - had been worth it.

I would like to extend my thanks to all my colleagues on the Comissão Pró-Resgate histórico da Ilha Anchieta.

TenenteSamuel

Author's Note

Antonio Braga is son of Private Geraldo Braga, who was part of the escort taking the prisoners to chop wood on the day of the rebellion.

Private Geraldo Braga was attacked by the prisoners with an axe; they smashed his head (with the rounded part, not the blade, luckily) and left him for dead.

He was found unconscious by other soldiers after the rebellion and taken to the doctor.

Two years later, as a result of the wounds he had received and which had left him psychologically damaged, he killed himself by swallowing poison.

He is a hero, a victim of the rebellion, even though his name does not appear in the official list, because he died two years later rather than on the day of the rebellion itself. (We intend to add his name on a monument to the heroes which is in front of the old Military detachment on the Morro de Papagaio).

Sergeant Theodosio Rodrigues dos Santos, who was with Private Braga when this happened, was also injured with an axe which battered in the bone in his forehead, and he had to live with this derormity all his life. I went to his funeral in Parque de Palmeiras cemetery in Gurilandia, Taubate, nearly three years ago.

One night, when I was swimming off the Praia do Sapateiro, looking back at the island, I began to wonder why exactly Anchieta fascinates people so much, and these verses came into my head.

Ilha Anchieta

Ilha Anchieta querida.
Recanto da minha vida
Quanta magia contida.
Quanta história vivida...

Qual é o seu segredo?
Por que a todos fascina?
Em seus mistérios o medo.
Em seus encantos ensina.

Tenente Samuel

When we are on the island, we feel a mysterious energy in the very air, the water, the rocks, the trees, in everything....it's as if it embraces and mesmerizes us. From that moment on, our senses are sharpened and our energy somehow interacts with that of the island.

You begin to feel that you'd like to stay.

And if we were to stay, we'd gradually begin to change, to become a bit Indian, a bit of a magician, a bit clairvoyant, a bit philosophical.

It becomes difficult to leave that place… to leave her.

Feel this on a sunny day, with the sky and the sea both blue, to start with.

Bits and pieces

1- Famous phrases:

"Se eu souber que uma mulher ou criança foi maltratada, o causador terá morte pelas minhas mãos. Nosso fim é a fuga". (João Pereira Lima).

"É necessário conhecer o sofrimento para avaliar a felicidade". (Preso n°. 436 Gauchão).

"Pode desembarcar, Coronel. O que tinha que acontecer já aconteceu". (Diretor Fausto Sady Ferreira, Diretor do Instituto Correcional da Ilha Anchieta- ICIA).

"A Ilha Anchieta não é de ninguém. É de todos nós". (Dr. Manoel de Azevedo Fontes).

The publication of this book has led to other pieces of work about the rebellion being written by academics in various different fields. Many university students are using the story of Anchieta as the subject of their PhD theses, Masters' dissertations etc. There are different books with different authors, focussing on different aspects. They have been inspired by this book just as I looked, and still look, for books which had been published before mine.

There are many things still to be revealed about the island.

Those who look with the necessary humility, if they are ready and if they are lucky will find things...

Replies to readers

The name of the young man, friendly with everybody and much-loved on the island, who was killed while fishing on the rocks of saco Grande in the 1950s, was Benedito Gabriel de Campos and was the godfather of Private José Salomão das Chagas' child.

Private José Salomão das Chagas was used as a hostage to get Lieutenant Odvaldo to surrender, after the prisoners had taken over the jail.

When the Lieutenant Paulo Vianna, Commander of the detachment 314, Ilha Anchieta, ordered the troops to beat up the prisoners in

Pavilhao 06, he did so because those prisoners had killed a colleague of his known as "Ze Pretinho". This contributed to PV's being called back to the battalion in Taubate. A Lieutenant who was more humane, according to some people, Lieutenant Odvaldo Silva, then replaced him as military commander of Ilha Anchieta.

- The expression "tomou um mofo" (to get mouldy) used on the island when the prison was there, meant a cold shower.
- Two sheets hanging out next to the "Spy Post" on the boqueirao, meant that visitors were either coming to or leaving the island. One sheet meant that there a prisoner had escaped.
- Private "Carioquinha" from the spy-post, saw who it was who swam across the Boqueirao, and it was Private Simao Rosa da Cunha. This can be confirmed by reading Carioquinha's correspondence.
- The fisherman Andrelino Miguel, arrived at the Boqueirao in his rowing boat at the moment of the rebellion and took some policeman across who later said that they had swum across too.
- In 1942, as the 1940 came into force, that Ilha Anchieta became the site of a maximum security prison called Instituto correctional da Ilha Anchieta-ICIA.

In all the books which I have read, the figure of 25 dead is mentioned and I agreed with that figure in earlier editions because there was no proof that the number was higher.

I now believe that the authorities hid the surprisingly high number of deaths. After the first edition of this book was published, I had a conversation with Antonio Francisco Alves, "Escoteiro", who had been sent to Anchieta prison at the age of only 17, even though he was not a criminal and had never been tried, and where he served three years. In the end, it was proved that he had committed no crime and he became a prison guard, and eventually the head of security of the prison. He was the biggest collaborator that the authorities had. He confided in me that, after the rebellion, when he was already head of security he checked the number of prisoners who had been re-captured and found that ninety were missing. Well, ninety plus the twelve prisoners and ten police officers who offi-

cially died, plus the six prisoners who disappeared makes 118......
- It continues to be the biggest prison rebellion the world has ever seen. This number was, however, camouflaged by the authorities at that time, and I know that there is no material evidence, but "Escoteiro" is a trustworthy person who was involved in the prison like no other. I have hesitated to mention this higher figure, but whenever I have talked about it in my speeches, many listeners, particularly those who have heard me at my book sales on the island itself, have urged me to make it public. The most recent was a client from the company DANA, Joelma by name, who was on Anchieta accompanied by dozens of employees of this multinational, and who all agreed with her, saying that I shouldn't leave this out of the second edition of the book. I have duly mentioned it, as they requested.

Carioquinha's correspondence

On the 7th June 2001, I received a phone call from sergeant Ref PM Manoel de Oliveira, asking me to go to number 9, Rua Parana in Taubate, where a document belonging to his brother Jose Benedito de Oliveira, "Carioquinha, was waiting for me.

When I arrived there a few minutes later, I got a wonderful surprise. Not only was the document there waiting for me, but also "Carioquinha" himself.

I order to remind readers who this important character is, I will just say a few words: Jose Benedito de Silva, known as "Carioquinha", was doing guard duty at the Spy Point (Posto do espia) which was on the other side of the Boqueirao, on the mainland itself, from where he could see the whole north coast of the island, the one which lies nearest the continent. When Private Simao Rosa da Cunha swam across from the island during the rebellion, "Carioquinha" was on duty, as I have said.

After we had introduced ourselves, we sat down at the table in his brother's house, had a cold drink and then had a lively conversation about the history of the island.

Carioquinha gave me a document, which he himself had signed, containing the story of his meeting with Simao.

Seeing how interested I was, he spoke of that moment, which was so emotional for him and which he has never forgotten.

I keep this document amongst my papers, from which I will now copy the following excerpt;

I was looking through the binoculars, to see if I could make out what was happening on the island. I could see that someone had dived into the sea and was swimming towards me. At that moment I thought it had to one of the fugitives, who had thrown himself into the sea in desperation, because the part he was swimming through was full of sharks, and only a person who was really desperate would risk his life in that way. As he got nearer, I ordered him, several times, to come up onto the rocks so that I could see who he was, because if he didn't I would have to shoot. The man who was swimming cried out.

"Don't shoot! It's me, Simao!

As I couldn't identify him straightaway, I repeated that he had to come up onto the rocks, as it was really difficult for me to believe that it was a military policeman, given that we all knew the great danger of swimming in those waters.

After this order, he got out of the water and I could see that it really was (the Soldier Simão Rosa da Cunha), who, exhausted, told me about the tragedy that was unfolding on the island as a result of the mutiny of the prisoners.

It has to be emphasised that the soldier Simão Rosa da Cunha acted extremely bravely, because, if he had been the kind of person who only thought of himself, he would have stayed hidden and no-one would have found him, but, knowing the problems his colleagues were confronting on the island, he decided to risk his life and swim over to the spy post to ask for help. Remember that the waters he swam through were full of sharks and that this action could only have been taken by a real hero."

In face of this written and spoken testimony, it is clear that the person who swam across the Boqueirão that day was none other than

Soldier Simão Rosa da Cunha.

The Governor's opinion

On the night of 19th April 2001, Alckmin decided to try and get to sleep by reading one of his books that didn't look too difficult, something light. He went to the bookshelf in his room and chose something that looked pleasant: a short book called Ilha Anchieta. He thought he was about to read a sweet and pleasant narrative, full of nice images. He was mistaken. He had chosen the book by Lieutenant Samuel Messias de Oliveira about the bloody rebellion on Anchieta in 1952. Twenty two prisoners and police (at least, that is the official number) died during an attempted escape which had taken five months to plan. He began to read and found he couldn't put it down till he'd read it all the way through. "Fifty years later, the only thing that's changed are the weapons they use", he said, "Instead of the mobile phones smuggled into prison of today, they used axes for chopping firewood".

Reportagem de Ricardo Kotscho na Revista Época n°. 145/2001.

Appendix to the third edition

Each year that goes by, more people who lived through the rebellion on Ilha Anchieta get in touch with us. Descendants of those survivors have also made themselves known to me, bringing me objects, photos and articles from that time, which show what a contrast there was between the apparent paradise of a beautiful tropical island, with the violence of the rebellion which took place there.

One of the texts sent to us was this song:

Enchanted isle
(Autoria desconhecida)

I feel in my soul
The song of this enchanted isle
Among the palm trees on the beach

In the sky, the Southern Cross
Where the stars shine
And the blue is more intense

Life is like
A dream of love
Forget your grief
And listen to the hurt

And then, what nostalgia
The place inspires
Of loved ones
So far across the sea

A song which the prisoners used to sing and which was given to me on 4th March 2003 by Ivone Villela Guadrix, (Daughter of the Island!").

What we feel on the island

The birdsong
The scent of the flowers
The sea breeze
The sound of the waves

The surf on the rocks
The clouds on the mountain ramparts
The blue of the sky reflected in the sea
The green of the foliage

The stories about the heroes and the bad men
The ruins of the works of Ramos de Azevedo
The manual work we all need to do
The breaking of our daily bread
Stories of ghosts and spaceships

The sacrifices we all make
Reflection in moments of solitude
Nostalgia for those who did not come this summer
Hoping to see tomorrow's sun.

Lieutenant Samuel

When I am on the island

Whenever I am on the island I feel as if I have come home.

Standing on the path which leads to Praia Grande (or Praia das Palmas) , I look out at sea towards the Boqueirao, and think that I did the same thing many, many years ago in a previous life; that is, I stood there meditating and looking out to sea.

Right in front of me is the dirt wall made of pebbles and stones, one on top of the other, which holds up the path.

Underneath, sloping a bit, is a block of solid stone, with parallel furrows, where the waves, after breaking, drain back into the sea. They seem to get stirred up in a kind of hollow and produce a special, low-pitched kind of sound.

Behind me is the Morro do Farol, which stands silently, majestically indifferent, with an air of eternal, imperturbable eternity.

Where are all my friends from that former life? Can it be that they are those who are working beside me? Why do I feel as if some friends are missing? Could it be the "Filhos da Ilha"?

And the "criminals"? What role do they play in my life?

Maybe they were pirates in that other life......

On my left, the Praia das Palmas, which used to be known as Praia Grande, extends for a kilometre, contrasting with the lush vegetation. I imagine how many bonfires there used to be at night, round which the Tupinamba warriors would gather and chat about the hunting, fishing or fighting they had done that day, fighting against the fierce white men of the "Capitania" of Sao Vicente…or the brave Tupiniquins of the Sao Paulo plateau.

How many stories lost to us would show what good warriors those men were who protected the top, most feared chief, the cacique Cunhambebe, the owner of that island which, over time, would give shelter to French sailors, and English and Portuguese soldiers? Later this island would become the diocese of Senhor Bom Jesus da Ilha dos Porcos. After that, the prison was established with its prisoners, employees, both military and civilian and now the island is the State park of Ilha Anchieta. And there I am thinking and looking for answers to all my questions.

Lieutenant Samuel

Prisoners participants of the rebellion of 1952

AGENOR MARQUES DE OLIVEIRA (Chocolate)
AGENOR PEREIRA DA COSTA (José Soldado)
ALCIDES DE SOUZA E SILVA
ALCIDES DOS SANTOS (Nariz de Negro)
ALCIDES SALDANHA (Zolhudo)
ALCINDO CÂNDIDO GOMES (Mocoroa)
ALMIR ALVES DA SILVA (Almirzinho ou Baiano da Faca)
ALVARO DA CONCEIÇÃO CARVALHO FARTO (Portuga) +
ANORELINO SORES (Capitão ou Capitão Sujeira)
ANTONIO DO CARMO (Antoninho)
ANTONIO HENRIQUE DA SILVA (Caipira)
ANTONIO MIGUEL FREIRE +
ARLINDO TORRES DA PAZ

....Total 13

BENEDITO CONCEIÇÃO FONTES
BENEDITO CORREIA DA SILVA (Mikimba)
BENEDITO RODRIGUES (Marigo Magro ou Mario ou Maluco)
BERNARDO ROSEMBERG
BRASIL MESTRE (Manolo)
DOMINGOS CUNHA
ESMERINDO BELMIRO DA SILVA (Pernambuco)
ETHEL PINHEIRO (Pinheirinho)
EURICO SILVA FILHO (Capitão Carnera)
FILADELFO MARTINS DE OLIVEIRA (Sacudo) +
FLORIANO PEDRO DA SLVA(Tabu)
FRANCISCO BARRIENTO +
FRACISCO JOSÉ DA SILVA (José da Silva ou Augusto cordeiro Rocha, Baianão) +
FLAVIO FERNANDES DA SILVA

GERALDO CAETANO (Passarinho)
GERALDO FRANCISCO DE OLIVEIRA (Negão da Cozinha)
GERALDO FONSECA DE SOUZA (Diabo Loiro)
HENRIQUE FRANCISCO GONÇALVES (Trovão)
HIDEO KIMAMOTO +
HILDEFONSO HOJAS (Vinte ou Vintinho)
IRINEU QUIRINO DOS SANTOS +
IRINEU SOUZA PRADO
JAIR INÁCIO ROSA (Mineirão)
JAIR PEREIRA (Vaqueirinho)
JOÃO ALVES DOS SANTOS (Swing)
JOÃO PEREIRA LIMA
JOÃO ROCHA
JOÃO SANTANA GAIA
JOÃO SEGISMUNDO BONOSO (Dr Bonoso)
JOAQUIM ALEXANDRE (Jerico)
JOAQUIM FARIAS (Cavalinho)
]JORGE FLORIANO (China Show)
JOSÉ ALVES TEIXEIRA FILHO (Barriquinha)
JOÉ ANTONIO GOMES (Carioca)
JOSÉ CÂMARA (Sapinho)
JOSÉ DA SILVA (Mambaia)
JOSÉ DA SILVA (Ritinha)
JOSÉ DA SILVA (Zelão)
JOSÉ DE MOURA (Zé Macaco)
JOSÉ FERNANDES DA SILVA (Zé Ozório)
JOSÉ GERALDO DE OLIVEIRA (Chatinho)
JOSÉ MIGUEL DOS SANTOS
JOSÉ NERY SANTANA
JOSÉ RODRIGUES DE ALMEIDA (Olhos Azuis)
JOSÉ VENÂNCIO DOS SANTOS (Bob)
JULIO ALVES (Cariocão)
LUIZ CARLOS LOPES (Luminoso)

LUIZ FARIA PADEIRO (Pedeirinho)
MANOEL AUGUSTO CAVALEIRO (Neco)
MANOEL VENÂNCIO DA SILVA (Embrulho)
MARIO PEREIRA DA SILVA
MAURÍCIO ANASTÁCIO
MAURO DELALIZ ou JOSÉ PIMENTEL (Alemãozinho)
MOACIR DE PAULA (Galo Cego)
NARCISO SILVA (Hermínio)
NELSON GARCIA
NILO PRADO ALVES
OSCAR KOSLOSKI (Oscarzinho)
OSCAR TEODORO DA SILVA (Mineirinho)
PEDRO FLORES GALANTE (Perico)
PEDRO JOAQUIM DOS SANTOS (Daziza ou Ziza)
ROBERTO SILVA JUNIOR
SEBASTIÃO GERMANO DOS SANTOS (Pavaozinho) +
SEBASTIÃO MANOEL DE SOUZA (Maluco)
SILVAL CABRAL DOS SANTOS (Gauchão)
VICENTE AMORIM (Xaxa)
VIRGOLINO MONTANA (Montanha)
WALDEMAR FERREIRA DA SILVA (Tiãozinho)
WILLIANS ALVES DA SILVA (Patolinha)
ZENON KIZON (Timochenko) +

.... Total 83 presos

List of prisoners recaptured close to Ubatuba, supplied to the newspaper "Última Hora" on june 23, 1952

Antonio Álvaro dos Santos nº. 11305;
Moacir Vasconcelos, 7850;
José de Moura, 10013;
Luis Farias Pacheco, 10900;

Manoel Antonio da Silva, 10613;
Osvaldo Soares, 554;
Grimaldo Ferreira, 575;
Manoel Venancio da Silva, 11455;
Benedito de Barros, 652;
Pedro Serafim dos Santos, 12019;
Roberto Silva Junior, 11592;
Sebastião Araújo, 729;
Julio Pereira da Cruz, 619;
Osvaldo de Souza, 699;
João Alves Filho, 674;
Monoel Marino de Castro, 8827;
José Alves da Silva, 681;
Mauro Higino Evangelista Moreira, 690;
Oscar Kasbevskin, 698;
Benedito Mateus de Carvalho, 655 e
Maurício Anastácio, 8100;

Arrested by the reporters of the "Última Hora"

José Fernandes da Silva, vulgo "Britador";
José Ferreira, vulgo "Caolho" e
Moacir de Paula, vulgo "Galo Cego".

Arrested wounded

Geraldo Fonseca de Souza, vulgo "Diabo Loiro", 11505;
José Câmara, 378 e
Alcides de Souza Silva, 11506;

Mortos ao serem aprisionados

Deiko Kiamoto;

Domingos da Cunha.

Funcionários e policiais na Ilha Anchieta
(Registro de 1952, 1953, 1954,1955 Arquivo Histórico do PEIA)

Transcrito do Livro de Registros de Funcionários Civis e Militares.

CIVIS

ABÍLIO FERREIRA DANTAS
ACEDINO DOS SANTOS
ADHEMAR SANTANA
ADRIANO SALOMÃO DE OLIVEIRA
AMARO LOURENÇO DE ARAUJO
AMÉRICO JOSÉ SANTI
ANASTÁCIO LOPES DE MOURA
ANASTÁCIO LOPES DE M. FILHO.
ANTENOR DE OLIVEIRA GODOY
ANTONIO FRANCISCO ALVES
ANTONIO GABRIEL CORREA
ANTONIO INOCENTE ROQUE FUNCIA
ANTONIO MARCONDES GIL
ANTONIO SCIPIÃO BARRETO
ARMANDO NERI
ARTHUR MILITÃO DE OLIVEIRA
ATÍLIO DOS SANTOS
AUSTÉRIO OLIVEIRA BARROS
BELTRAN LOPES PESTANA
BENEDITO ALVES BARRETO
BENEDITO BENTO DE TOLEDO
BENEDITO CURSINO
BENEDITO DA SILVA (Peitudo)
BENEDITO DE ANDRADE

BENEDITO DE OLIVEIRA
BENEDITO DOS SANTOS
BENEDITO GABRIEL
BENEDITO GABRIEL DE CAMPOS
BENEDITO GONÇALVES SANTANA
BENEDITO GREGÓRIO
BENEDITO JOSÉ DOS SANTOS
BENEDITO NASCIMENTO CASTRO
BENEDITO RODRIGUES DE OLIVEIRA
BENEDITO SANTOS
BENEDITO VEIGA
BENTO AMANCIO
CARLOS GARCIA DA SILVA
CASEMIRO PRADO
CLAUDIO DE OLIVEIRA
DEOLINDO FELIPE DA SILVA
EDUARDO FERREIRA LISBOA
ESTÉFANO COBIAK
EUCLIDES VIEIRA
EUGÊNIO RUIZ
EURÍPEDES SANCHES MELO
FELISBINO TEODORO DA SILVA
FLAVIO DE TOLEDO LARA
FLORIVAL DE CASTRO
FRANCISCO FARIA JUNIOR
FRANCISCO SILVA CRUZ
FRANCISCO PAULINO DA SILVA
GABRIEL DE FORNISSET
GABRIEL VINHAS
GERALDO ANTUNES
GERALDO DOS SANTOS
GERALDO GALVÃO
GERALDO JOSÉ DA SILVA

GERMANO A. DOS SANTOS
GERÔNCIO ALVES CORREA
GERVÁSIO ALVES CORREA
GILBERTO BARBOSA
GONÇALINO DE DEUS
HAROLDO DE OLIVEIRA SILVA
HELÁDIO CRESPO ou
HELADIR CRESPO (HELÁDIO, afirmou Moraes de Faria)
HÉLIO CARDOSO DE BARROS
HIGINO PERES DE OLIVEIRA
HOLANDO OLIVEIRA
HORÁCIO JOSÉ FERREIRA
HORLANDO DE OLIVEIRA
IRINEU MOYSÉS DE OLIVEIRA
ITAGIR DOS SANTOS
JANIEL PINHEIRO
JOÃO ALVES DE ALMEIDA
JOÃO BASÍLIO RODRIGUES
JOÃO BATISTA ALVES
JOAQUIM FERREIRA DA SILVA
JOSÉ ABEL DA GRAÇA
JOSÉ ABÍLIO SHESQUE
JOSÉ BATISTA RAMOS
JOSÉ BENEDITO DA SILVA
JOSÉ BENEDITO DOS SANTOS
JOSÉ BENEDITO FABIANO
JOSÉ BENEDITO PEREIRA
JOSÉ BORDINI DO AMARAL
JOSÉ DA COSTA FERREIRA
JOSÉ DA SILVA (Pião)
JOSÉ DE SOUZA PINTO
JOSÉ FRANCISCO DOS SANTOS
JOSÉ GOMES VIEIRA

JOSÉ GONÇALVES SANTANA
JOSÉ LEITE MORAES
JOSÉ MARQUES DOS SANTOS
JOSÉ M. DA SILVA FILHO.
JOSÉ MENDES DA SILVA FILHO
JOSÉ MORENO RODRIGUES (RADIOTELEGRAFISTA)
JOSÉ TEIXEIRA PINTO
JOÃO ABÍLIO SHERQUE
JOÃO ALVES DE ALMEIDA
JOÃO BALBINO DOS SANTOS
JOÃO BATISTA
JOÃO COSTA FERREIRA
JOÃO DA COSTA FERREIRA
JOÃO DIAS DE ABREU (Médico)
JOÃO RODOLFO CABRAL DOS SANTOS
JOÃO RODOLFO CAHOL DOS SANTOS
JOAQUIM FERREIRA DA SILVA
JUAREZ FERREIRA CARDOSO
JULIO FRANCISCO PEREIRA
LUIZ ALVES MOREIRA
LUIZ ARANTES
LUIZ BATISTA LIMA
LUIZ BATISTA DE LIMA
LUIZ FERREIRA CUNHA
LUIZ GUILHERME DE OLIVEIRA
LUIZ MARIA DE SOUZA
MANOEL ALBINO
MANOEL CARVALHO MADEIRA
MAN OEL DA COSTA FERREIRA
MANOEL ELPÍDIO DA SILVA
MANOEL FERREIRA LISBÔA
MANOEL LOPES SAMPAIO
MARIA DAS DORES BARBOSA (PROFESSORA)

MARIO AMARAL
MARTINS FERREIRA
NATANAEL DE AQUINO
NÉLIO CARDOSO DE BARROS
NELSON DE JESUS
NERCÍLIO JOÃO DE LIMA
NOEL MIZAEL
ODETE SERPA (Professora)
OSWALDO DOS SANTOS (Fairbanks)
OSVALDO SIMÕES
PAULO GABRIEL CORREA
PEDRO DE MORAES CLARO
PEDRO FERREIRA DOS SANTOS
PEDRO FRANCISCO DOS SANTOS
PEDRO LUCAS FERREIRA
PEDRO MORAIS CLARO
PEDRO OLIVEIRA MACHADO
PORTUGAL DE SOUZA PACHECO
ROMÃO LUIZ MOREIRA
ROQUE ALVES DE TOLEDO
ROSA CUBA DE SOUZA
SEBASTIÃO FERNANDES FARIA
TARCISO GALVÃO LUIZ
TEREZA ROSA PARCIZE
VENÂNCIO PAIVA FILHO
VITOR LOPES
WALDEMAR FRANCISCO AMARAL
WALTER ALVES

MILITARES

SOLDADO AFONSO RIBAS CESAR
SARGENTO ANGELO GERALDO

SARGENTO ANTENOR ALVES DE SÁ
SOLDADO ANTENOR DE OLIVEIRA GODOY
CABO ANTENOR VAZ DE CAMPOS
SOLDADO ANTONIO DE PAULA MOREIRA
SOLDADO ANTONIO MARCELINO RIBEIRO
SOLDADO ANTONIO MARCONDES GIL
SOLDADO ANTONIO R. GARCIA FILHO
SOLDADO ARTUR MILITÃO DE OLIVEIRA
SOLDADO BENEDITO A. FERREIRA FILHO
SOLDADO BENEDITO DAMÁSIO DOS SANTOS
SOLDADO BENEDITO DE OLIVEIRA
CABO BENEDITO GERALDO
SOLDADO BENEDITO GREGÓRIO
SOLDADO BENEDITO LUIZ DOS SANTOS
SOLDADO BENEDITO MOREIRA
SOLDADO BENEDITO DA SILVA (O Setecentos)
SOLDADO BENTO MOREIRA
TENENTE CÂNDIDO ANTONIO REGO (Tenente)
SOLDADO CARMO DA SILVA (Cavalaria)
SARGENTO CHERUBIM DE LIMA FRANCO
SALDADO DARCY VARGAS
SOLDADO DIÓGENES DA SILVA (Pernambuco)
SOLDADO EDUARDO SENE
SOLDADO ESTÉFANO COBIAH
SOLDADO EUGÊNIO PADUAN
Cap Res EB FAUSTO SADY FERREIRA (Diretor)
SARGENTO FRANCISCO GONÇALVES
SOLDADO FRANCISCO PAULINO DA SILVA
SOLDADO GERALDO BRAGA
CABO GERALDO DOS SANTOS
SOLDADO GERALDO SEBASTIÃO DOS SANTOS
SOLDADO GONÇALINO DE DEUS
CABO HILÁRIO ROSA

SARGENTO HUGO RIBEIRO DIAS
SOLDADO JOÃO ABÍLIO FILHO
SOLDADO JOÃO BASÍLIO RODRIGUES
SOLDADO JOÃO BATISTA
CABO JOÃO RIBEIRO DE CASTILHO
SOLDADO JOAQUIM FERREIRA DA SILVA
SOLDADO JONI DE CAMPOS
TENENTE JONAS SIMÕES MACHADO
SOLDADO JOSÉ ANTONIO DOS SANTOS
SOLDADO JOSÉ AUGUSTO DA CONCEIÇÃO
SOLDADO JOSÉ BENEDITO DE OLIVEIRA
SOLDADO JOSÉ BENEDITO PEREIRA
SOLDADO JOSÉ CARNEIRO GARCIA
SOLDADO JOSÉ DA CUNHA GOUVEIA
CABO JOSÉ DE ALMEIDA
SOLDADO JOSÉ DE OLIVEIRA NETO
SOLDADO JOSÉ EUGÊNIO O PADUAN
SOLDADO JOSÉ FERREIRA DIAS
SOLDADO JOSÉ GOMES VIEIRA
SOLDADO JOSÉ LAURINDO
SOLDADO JOSÉ MARIA
SOLDADO JOSÉ SALOMÃO DAS CHAGAS
CABO JOSÉ SUDÁRIO FRANCO
SOLDADO JOSÉ TEODORO DE PAULA
SOLDADO LUCAS GONÇALVES DO PRADO
SOLDADO LUIZ ALVES MOREIRA
SOLDADO LUIZ VITÓRIO LIMA FILHO
SOLDADO MANOEL FRANÇA AYRES
SOLDADO MANOEL LEME
SOLDADO MANOEL VIEIRA NOVAES
SOLDADO MARTINIANO FÁBIO
SARGENTO MELCHIADES ALVES DE OLIVEIRA
SOLDADO MELTIADES BERTOLDO ALVES

SOLDADO NELSON DE JESUS
CABO NICANOR RAMALHO
SOLDADO NOEL MISAEL
SOLDADO OCTÁVIO DOS SANTOS
TENENTE ODWALDO SILVA
SOLDADO PAULO GABRIEL CORREA
SOLDADO PEDRO LEITE
SOLDADO SEBASTIÃO BARRETO DA SILVA
SOLDADO SEBASTIÃO FERNANDES FARIA
SOLDADO SEBASTIÃO TEODORO DA SILVA
SOLDADO SIMÃO ROSA DA CUNHA
SARGENTO TEODÓSIO RODRIGUES DOS SANTOS
CABO WALDOMIRO DE MATOS OLIVEIRA
CABO WALTER CARDOSO
SOLDADO VITOR AMÂNCIO DE FARI

About the Trainees' song

In summer, after 7pm , when the last tourists have left the island, the trainees find themselves alone and, their work having finished, free until 7am the next morning.

The first thing they do is go into the sea for a refreshing dip. After their swim and a shower, they go to eat dinner and wait for the time to go to bed.

They are all young people, and always get together in the evenings at some pretty spot to sing and play their guitars.

They sing the saddest, most nostalgic songs.

Sometimes they liven up the music with a couple of tambourines, cow bells and even berimbaus.

On one of those evenings, I heard this song:

Days of January
(by Leandro Rezende, Marcelo Areco and Morcegada)

I still remember those January days
The crowd on the pier waiting for the schooner,
The whole day long……

I am not going to wash the mirror
And don't ask me to clean the bathroom!
Because I have to work with tourists
The whole day long.

January days
January days

The daily grind
A slave's life
Stitching away all day like a fool!

Maria Bonita arriving
127 nego shouting
I am not the one who's going to speak to them
I am at the drawing board

Ilha anchieta
Ilha Anchieta

I eat dry bread every day
There is a pile of washing up in the sink
I've still got to polish up my CV
And here comes Maria…..

Conga is in the Boqueirao

But what a dog's life I lead
There's no time for a good shower
And I am not going South cos I am in sandals….

If someone tells me to clean up capybara poo
I say this is stupid
But no-one believes me
Here I go to the compost heap

Tourists running away from the wasps
Just making me laugh
These great big black things
They never hurt anybody!

I am tired of saying
That the Tamar project is no longer here
If you want to see turtles
Then go to Itagua!

Eta, eta, eta
Ilha Anchieta
Eta, eta, eta
Ilha Anchieta (2x)

Pirate

One of the most famous pirates spent sometime here along the coast of Brazil. His name: Thomas Cavendish. He was born in Trimley St Martins, near Ipswich, Suffolk in 1555. He studied at Corpus Christi College, at the University of Cambridge. He was given a special honour by Queen Elizabeth I.

On account of his bravery and fearlessness, he was made a general at the young age of just 31, with instructions to attack Spanish ships wherever he should find them. He was by now a very rich man and he turned down the advantages and privileges of the job, as well as the financial backing of the government, preferring to work for himself.

He equipped three ships with crews of criminals and lots of arms and ammunition. In southern waters, he laid siege to the Spanish ships with their cargoes of gold and precious stones, which they had got from the indigenous peoples by bartering mirrors, knives, cheap jewellery and other bits and bobs. Those "floating trunks" belonging to the Spanish were "liberated "of their cargo as they were returning to Europe, by the English pirates.

From time to time Cavendish returned to London, where he was treated like a real hero. His followers, the lowest of the low, covered with filth and fleas, began to show off, wearing fine clothes, gold jewellery and precious stones.

The white sails of the captain's ship were changed for brocade ones and the hull of the ship was decorated with rare metals. He was known as a perverse, strange man as a result of these strange customs.

He led an attack on Santos and Sao Vicente at Christmas 1592, when most of the people were at midnight Mass, and his men looted and then burned all the houses.

Antonio Alvares Filho, the historian from Santos, wrote many times in his columns for the newspaper A Tribuna de Santos about Cavendish, saying that it was possible that the lost treasure of the pirate was buried in the Ilha da Moela, in front of the bay of Santos.

The pirate would have decided to put the treasure he had got from this looting somewhere safe. He chose five sailors, lowered a boat down into the water, and, without their weapons, they transported everything overland; he told the sailors it was ammunition that they were hiding...One of the five sailors chosen was the Englishman Taylor, a fugitive from justice and, like his boss, after easy money.

On leaving the ships, they rowed for along time until they reached the Ilha Da Moela, where the sailors carried the trunks full of treasure along a path to a place that had been chose, well inland. There, on Cavendish's orders, they dug a deep hole to bury the treasure. Taylor was supposed to stay behind, keeping an eye on the launch, but, not trusting his captain, he tied up the boat and followed at a distance, without being seen. When they had buried the trunks of treasure, the sailors, tired and unarmed, offered no resistance when Cavendish attacked them with his sword. He killed all four of them and buried them alongside the trunks full of treasure. Taylor, still hidden, turned around quickly and went back to the boat where he waited for Cavendish.

When Cavendish got back, Taylor asked him what had happened to the four who had not returned. Cavendish, annoyed, replied that they had been attacked by natives and that only he had managed to escape. Taylor rowed the boat back towards the ship. As they got near, Taylor realised he was in a difficult situation and that things could get even worse for him and so he threw himself into the sea and swam to the Ilha de Santo Amaro, from where he fled to Sao Paulo de Piratininga, which is today the city of Sao Paulo. He stayed there, got married and worked as an excellent blacksmith, until one day nostalgia for his old life overwhelmed him and he took off for the Ilha da Moela to look for the treasure.

Without a map and after so many years away from the island, Taylor had no luck and got older and older but he didn't give up and continued looking. One day, exhausted, he died on the island. He hadn't been able to find the treasure that he had helped his old captain take there.

The writer Cicero Baurk, in his interesting book, "ilhabela e seus misterios" refers to Cavendish, saying that he always returned to Ilhabela after his attacks on the Spanish, to celebrate and to make new plans of attack.

A mutiny on board ship in the high seas, after an epidemic of scurvy, led to Cavendish being hanged from the main mast of his ship. The mutineers, as soon as they returned to the island, sank the ships.

The treasures which Cavendish buried are still being searched for today in Ilhabela and in Trindade, which is between Ubatuba and parati, that is, the dividing line between the state of Sao Paulo and the state of Rio de Janeiro. Another famous coastal writer, whom I had the pleasure to meet in person, Washington de Oliveira, the "Filinho da farmacia", in his book "Ubatuba, Legends and other stories" (TRANSLATE) believed that "the treasure of Thomas Cavendish exists and must be here in the north of the Ubatuba municipality, in a bay along the coast called Caxadaco. Caxadaco is obviously a corruption of "Caixa de aço" (Box of steel), in which the CORSARIO Thomas Cavendish hid his treasures".

He continues, "Did Cavendish die off the coast of Pernambuco, as the enciclopédia Delta Larousse says, or near Ascension Island, as Antonio Álvares Filho tells us, or was he hanged on his ship near Ilhabela, as Cícero Buark implies". He makes one further observation, "One more thing: in the Ilha Anchieta, which used to be called Ilha dos Porcos, if you go along the trail which leads from Praia Grande to Praia do Sul, and go slightly off the path just before you get there, you will see a rough, rectangular cement slab, which clearly has in its four corners deep holes, as if to hold candles. At the head of this stone is another stone, this one is upright, with a shape hollowed out in the form of a cross; the whole thing gives the impression of being a gravestone of some kind.

Could Cavendish have died on the coast or on one of the islands of the state of Sao Paulo? Could he have been buried on the Ilha Anchieta? Could his followers have showed him respect by marking his grave in this way, in a corner of an isolated beach?".

Acknowledgements and thanks

In November 2006, Dra Viviane C. Buchianeri, the director of the State Park of Ilha Anchieta, asked me to choose fifteen of the Children of the Island (Filhos da Ilha) to attend a course in order to train them how to welcome guests to the island in summer.

I was able to find only eleven who would have time to do this work, and of these eleven, eight finished the course and became PEIA monitors. Their names are:

CELI DOS SANTOS GIRAUD;

CÉLIO SALES DEALMEIDA;

DIONÉIA DA CRUZ;

IARA RIBEIRO DIAS;

JOSÉ SALOMÃO DAS CHAGAS;

LIA BURDINI AMARAL;

MARIANA ROSA DA CUNHA;

CABO ALMEIDA;

WALTINHO CARDOSO;

EDISON PRADO "RISCADINHO;

NATALICE PRADO.

It is clear how important they are. Tourists feel very lucky to have contact with the actual survivors of the rebellion, and their descendants, who can talk about how it really was to be there in the 1950s. The words of Luiz Felipe de Azevedo, the Municipal Secretary of Tourism in Ubatuba, were published in various newspapers, "Ilha Anchieta is to Ubatuba what the Sugar Loaf Mountain cable-car is to Rio de Janeiro". Rene, one of the councillors of the Municipal Council for Tourism in Ubatuba, says, "Ilha Anchieta is a unique Ubatuba tourist destination".

The teacher Dioneia da Cruz, who was born on the island, daughter of one of the workers at the prison, Senhor Chico Cruz, and his wife, Rita, became a symbol of the survivors when her photo, one of several of the children of the island, was taken the day after the rebellion, and later published, by the magazine "O Cruzeiro". The photo is re-published here, in this book. On the day the photo was taken, Dioneia was seven years old and one of the children who attended the little school on the island, along with her class-mate Celio Sales de Almeida. She met up with him 54 years later on the Training Course I have mentioned. He is the class-mate who is referred to in the poem "A Volta" (Return)", which I have printed below.

After her first summer as a monitor, which was a complete success, Dioneia has stayed on the island from Thursday to Monday every week. The others who finished the training course return to the island every June for our annual meeting, to help us organise the events for the other Filhos da ilha, and also go back every summer (January) to continue working as receptionists for the visitors and to keep the historic paths open.

The Return

by Dioneia (Preta)

On hot nights, wrapped up in memories
I dream of returning to the island
On waking, I face the harsh reality
Of maybe never going back.

But shown the way by dear friends
Mara, Heloiza, Viviane and Samuel
I fulfil my life's dream
Divine angels sent by God!

Sailing though the white surf
The boat follows its normal course;
As we come round into the Boqueirao
I search for a glimpse of my native land.

As the scene is illuminated on the horizon
Bathed in sunshine, a rare delight
Childhood memories flood back
Overcoming me with bitter-sweet tears

Like a prodigious mother in a happy fairy tale
With open arms towards the sea
My beloved island waits tirelessly, serenely
Hoping to see her daughter return!

On this soil, with small, wandering steps
I go to the sacred places of my childhood
And hear the ballads of that time
And meet again a friend from my infancy

Hand in hand, feeling the same emotion,
I let the past sweep over me as I weep
And Mother Island, in her lullaby
Rocks my memories and dreams

I thank God for this return
He preserved this a long time for me
Like a Father offering his daughter
A new family to love

Ubatuba, 22/07/08
Dionéia

Foto of the author of this bock, Lieutenant Samuel Messias.

Agradecimentos e Bibliografia

Acknowledgements
(Abreviaturas militares)

We are grateful for the support that has been given to us by the Commanders Cel Nelson Francisco Duarte, Paulo Cesar Máximo, José Antono Rosa, Lamarque Monteiro, Maj Eugênio Cesário Martins, as well as the President of the Association of Retired Police officers in Taubate, Captain Wilson Prado Palma, and the President of the Corporals and Privates of Taubate, Milton Vieira and the Directors Corporal Jorge and Corporal Santinho.

Presidente da Associação de SubTen e Sargentos-Regional Taubaté-, SubTen Sodré e os Diretores Tenente Martins e Sargento Nanci também membros ativos dessa Comissão. Agradecimentos reiterados ao Diretor do Parque Estadual da Ilha Anchieta Dr. Manoel de Azevedo Fontes e sua esposa Maria de Jesus Robim, bióloga responsável pelo Programa de Uso Público e Educação Ambiental da Ilha Anchieta.

À Cida Machado, responsável pelo levantamento patrimonial do Presídio da Ilha Anchieta, após seu fechamento.

Ao Dr. José Luiz de Carvalho, Coordenador de Informações Técnicas e Pesquisa do Instituto Florestal e Coordenador dos 12 Parques Estaduais da Região do Vale do Paraíba e Litoral Norte, inclusive o Parque Estadual da Ilha Anchieta.

Ao Dr. Ailton Barbosa Figueira, Diretor Regional de Economia e Planejamento do Vale do Paraíba e Litoral Norte, do Governo de Geraldo Alckmin.

A escritora Angela Galvão, de Pindamonhangaba.

Ao Prefeito Zizinho Vigneron de Ubatuba e seus assessores.

Ao Tenente Res PM. José Roberto Lamosa Chefe de Gabinete e Lenina, Relações Públicas.

Ao Prefeito Paulo Ramos e seus assessores.

Ao Prefeito Eduardo César e seus assessores.

Administração da Ilha: Dr². Viviane Buchianeri e Heloiza Folegatti, Cláudio Moreno de Barros, Tiago Martins, Dr². Maria de Jesus Robim, Odete. Valmir, Mario, Esbruzi, Tobias, Zé Pedro, Balio, Zé do Prado, Messias e aos irmãos: Pedro e Luiz, Isaias, Bitico e às cozinheiras Odete e Maria, Mara, Nanci e Nilda.

Monitores Ambientais do PEIA: Maycon Thomas, Larissa, Elias J. Santos, Claudinei, Marcelo, Reginaldo, Thiago Martins, Bira, Fernanda, Vânia, Cristina, Aline, Leandro, Mariana, Felipe, Carlinhos, Tâmara, Marília, Felipe Oliviere, Sergio Giovani (Gê), Marcelo Lopes Mota e Marcelo Areco Rosana, Cristiano, Cristina e Ely. Seguranças: Zico, Carlinos, Hercules, Renê, Valdemir, Alessandro,

Do Instituto da Pesca: P.Robinho e Zuleica.

Aos proprietários da Mykonos Turismo, Sr. Jean, Alexandre, e Áurea.

Aos funcionários: Norma, Tércio, Barnei, Trapezunda, Silvana, Ademir, André, Nei, Fabiana, Tais, Mara, Isabel, Roni, Ricardo, João, e Mônica. Marinaldo, "Burrico", Moacir e todos os demais componentes.

Da Corsário: Toninho, Junior, Alemão Ricardo, Tânea, Adriano, Thiago, Ericson, Alexandre Alecty, Cíntia, Junior, Fabiano, Rogério, Marcela, Jô, Jaqueline e demais componentes.

Da Escuna Kalaine: Cesar e Davi.

Da Escuna Cap Denis: Ernani e Heloisa Rodrigues.

Da Escuna Black Fim: Marquinhos.

Da Escuna Fernanda: Roberto Ferrari.

Da Escuna Vulcano: Eduardo e Edmundo.

Da Escuna Paraguaçu: Nakata.

Da Escuna Ubatur: Sr. Nícolas Evângelos;

Do Projeto Tamar: Hélio, Jane e Carla.

Do Restaurante das Estrelas: Patrícia, neta do saudoso Chico Maciel, Itá, Walter, Waldir e Vinicius.

Da rua Maciel, no continente: Ivete Maciel, filha do Chico Maciel.

A Lilian Prado Santos, esposa do vereador Osmar.

Ao vereador Osmar e assessores.

A Marlene e a Vivian.

Aos grandes colaboradores Arthur Nerer e Luciana.

Thanks to the Press

To the radio announcers Jura Belo and Sanches, who were seen in Ubatuba , and who have attended all the great gatherings we have had and which have been mentioned in this book, and whose work has helped to spread word about the events.

À Rede de Jornais Associados: José Antonio de Oliveira, Renato Campos, Luiz Carlos, Alex, Adriano, Paola, Kátia Dubsky, Deniele Simões e Daniela Bairros. À senhora Nadir, Adélia, Fátima, Raul Ribas, Neon e Maria, Hugo Nóbrega, Simões de Carvalho e João Monteiro, Robertinho, Cruel, Marinho e Michel, com os quais trabalhamos há muitos anos. João Paulo Ouvernei, Lucas e Thais.

À TV Setorial: Laura Barcha, Luiz Carlos, Gislene, Miguel, Maurílio Laua, Magda, Rodrigo Vilela e Carol.

À Voz do Vale, Semana de Ubatuba, Gazeta da Estiva, Informativo "Clarinadas da Tabatinguera" da AORPM.

À Rádio Difusora: Nagib Kalil, Percy Lacerda, Walter Magui, Pepe, Pedro Luiz, Chico de Paula, Rafael Lima, e Reinaldo Barbosa.

À FM 94,5: Sônia Grin, Julinho Pantera, Marcelo Pirani e Mirandinha.

À Rádio Cacique: Tenente Rangel.

À Rádio Rehma FM: Frank Cesar.

À Rádio Super Pop: Luciano.

À Rede Globo (TV Vanguarda): Levy Soares, Stela, Hélio Rodrigues, Pedro Mantoan, Araquem, Odair e Herivelton.

Aos Apresentadores do SPTV: Evaristo Rodrigues e Michele Costa.

À Semana de Ubatuba: Josias (Jija), Baltazar Nunes Sabóia, Francisco Carlos de Toledo e Inês de Sá.

À Voz do Vale: Ivani Senna e Ariane Ferreira.

À Folha Vale: Roger e Maurício.

Ao jornal "O Tempo": Ocimar Barbosa.

Bibliography

Facts collected from the books "A Ilha Anchieta e Eu" and "O Levante", by the late Colonel Paulo Vianna.

Sentença de Pronúncia…..

Facts from the book "O Salto na Amazônia" by the historian and writer Colonel Edilberto de Oliveira Melo, given to me by Cap Wilson Prado Palma.

Photos from the magazine "O Cruzeiro" of 1952, fondly kept for 46 years by the Senhora Brasilina Bretherick da Silva and her daughter Maria das Gracas (wife and daughter of Private Eugenio, of the Ilha Anchieta barracks) and kindly given to me for this book.

The book "Motim da Ilha", by the famous writer, teacher and Police Chief Benedito Nunes Dias. This was the first work about the mutiny that I came across and which inspired me, 23 years later, to publish three print runs of our magazine "Noticias Policiais" (Vale de Paraiba and northern coast of Sao Paulo edition).

Also exceedingly useful, were the statements of Senhora Gracia Palma and Senhora Aydee Cardoso, who lived on the island at the time of the mutiny, and the statement of Sergeant Afonso Alves, who was a Private on Ilha Anchieta in 1952.

Thanks also to the film-maker Private Afonso Alves Junior of the 5th BPMI, who accompanied us to the island in 1998 and filmed the excursion.

Thanks also to the island official, Antonio Francisco Alves, known as "Escoteiro", Sergeant Chagas and "Santo Cristo" We have also heard the testimonies of 100 survivors, some children, some adults at the time of the rebellion, and the testimonies of 248 families with whom we have made contact for the annual 20th June anniversary commemorations.

Thanks also to Arthur Neher and Luciana.

Additional Material

"Coracões Sujos" by Fernando Moraes (book)
"Imigração no Brasil" by Jorge Cocicov
"Mãos Sangrentas" by Cinema Company Maristela (film, 1952)

This work had its graphic design and layout developed by the journalist and Graphic Designer Cleyton Carlos Torres, compound types in Times New Roman PS MT e Times New Roman I, sizes 9, 10, 11, 12, 14 e 18.